Zionism, An Indigenous Struggle
Aboriginal Americans and the Jewish State

AN INDIGENOUS STRUGGLE

ABORIGINAL AMERICANS AND THE JEWISH STATE

edited by
Nathan Elberg
Machla Abramovitz

RVP Press New York
CIJR Montreal

RVP Publishers Inc. / RVP Press
Roslyn, New York

© 2020 / RVP Publishers Inc., Roslyn

All rights reserverd. No part of this book may be reproduced in any form or by any electronic or mechanical means, including information storage and retrieval systems, without persmission in writing from the publisher, except by a reviewer who may quote brief passages in a review.

RVP Press™ is an imprint of RVP Publishers Inc., Roslyn.

The RVP Publishers logo is a trademark of RVP Publishers Inc., Roslyn.

The publication of this book was supported by International Center for Western Values, Amsterdam in conjunction with the Canadian Institute for Jewish Research, Montreal.

The Canadian Institute for Jewish Research (CIJR) is an independent and internationally-known academic think-tank based in Montreal and Toronto. Its research focusses mainly on Israel, Jewish and Middle Eastern Issues. Staffed by respected, academic Fellows, the Institute aims to bring objective data and analysis of Israel, the Middle East, and Jewish-related issues to students—Jewish and non-Jewish, on and off campus—and to the media and government.

Library of Congress Control Number: 2019948423

ISBN 978 1 61861 342 4

www.rvppress.com

Table of Contents

7   **Machla Abramovitz**
Foreword

13   **Nathan Elberg**
Introduction

20   **Allen Z. Hertz**
Aboriginal Rights of the Jewish People

107   **Sally F. Zerker**
Israeli "Occupation": The BIG LIE

114   **Mara Cohen**
What it Means to Be an Oglala Sioux Jewish Woman:
A Personal Account

122   **Nathan Elberg**
Simple Truths: A Cree Indian Explains
a 2,000 Year Old Rabbinic Teaching

129   **Ira Robinson**
The David Ahenakew Affair and the Problem of Using
the Canadian Justice System in the Fight Against Antisemitism

144 Scott Benlevi
I Walk Two Worlds

148 Ryan Bellerose
Conversation With a Métis About Israel

154 Howard I. Schwartz
Savage and Jew: A Shared Stereotype

169 Dr. David A. Yeagley
There is no Palestine, There are no Palestinians

178 Jay Corwin
The Convergence of the Native American and Jewish Narratives in our Times

187 Ambassador Alan Baker
The Indigenous Rights of the Jewish People

192 Mara Cohen
Indians at Work

196 Uqittuk Mark, as told to Machla Abramovitz
Uqittuk Mark: Inuit Defender of Israel

201 Jose Faur
Jews, *Conversos,* and Native Americans: The Iberian Experience

225 Select Bibliography

Foreword

How is one's indigenous connection to a land expressed? For many Jews, it is by reclaiming their ancestral land after centuries of exile. Despite the political turmoil greeting Jews there and which remains a constant struggle, the land welcomed these early pioneers back with open arms. Its very soil responded to their touch and care: Its deserts bloomed and continues even today to produce and develop, providing not only for the needs of its residents but for a world that is increasingly partaking in its technological development and growth. As well, Israelis created a democracy that is open and free, and yet decidedly Jewish. However, Israel's need to integrate an ancient culture with the ever-evolving needs of a modern society remains a constant challenge. Within this multicultural society, issues of identity persist not only in the political sphere but the religious and cultural ones, as well. Despite these challenges, Israelis retain a strong sense of identity borne of a deep-rooted religious culture and value system realized to its fullest on the fertile soils of their ancestral homeland.

Unfortunately, the same cannot be said about many Aboriginal

Americans. Scattered across North America in their ancestral lands, many struggle to rediscover their "real selves" within societies—Aboriginal and nonaboriginal—whose way of life remains far removed from their ancient ways. In a 1984 paper he delivered at the 4th Inuit Studies Conference in Montreal, co-editor Nathan Elberg quoted the poignant words of a young Inuk (Eskimo) that well-articulated his people's struggles, which continue to this day.

> That Inuit culture had certain values that it inevitably was going to lose. We are in the process of losing it completely. We seem to be heading in a direction where everything is being computerized, where everything [is moving towards] the space age. So if we want to survive, we had better be a part of that system. It's so sad, but that's the way it is. Even the oldest Inuk today, even though not entirely Inuk, I call him Inuk, even though other people call him Inuk, even though he claims that he is Inuk, that does not give him the right to call me "qalluna" [white man]. He's right in some respects, but I can counterattack him by saying that he has lost his culture also because his father was greater than him. It's like saying the past was the best, and the future is the worst.

For Elberg, this collection of essays synthesizes two distinct political and social cultures that are deeply meaningful to him: Zionism, which is rooted in his Jewish upbringing, and that of Aboriginal Americans, many of whom he came to know and appreciate personally. As an anthropologist, he not only studied aboriginal culture but experienced it, as well: In the 1970s and 1980s, he lived amongst the Cree Indians in the Quebec North's James Bay region; the Eskimos in the Quebec North's Hudson Bay region; and among the Inuit of Labrador. He maintains friendships with several of them.

One of his most extended stays was during the frigid winter of 1981. While doing fieldwork in the James Bay region for a research project, he resided with Bobby, one of his Cree friends and his extended family—they were 17 to a "mijwap" (tipi)—about 500 miles from the nearest road. They lived in the forest and were dependent on hunting and fishing for their sustenance. Elberg didn't have any expectations as to what it would be like living there. "It was just a matter of experiencing it. It was a different way of life; it was a different way of looking at life. It was more a matter of direct experience of the world, rather than experiencing the world as mediated by a philosophy."

Several years before—in November 1975—the governments of Canada and Quebec and representatives of the Cree signed the James Bay and Northern Quebec Agreement that financially compensated them for the governments' hydroelectric development on Cree lands, and gave them limited rights and protection. Because the land was to be flooded to accommodate a newly-built dam, Bobby's family decided to trap all the fur-bearing animals possible reasoning that since the animals were going to die anyway, it was best to harvest their meat for food and pelts for sale. The Cree, Elberg explains, didn't see this as a business opportunity; rather, as an extension of their way of life, since hunting animals is part of the Crees' everyday experience. This experience starts early: The baby girl residing in their tipi nonchalantly played with her toy—a dead rabbit.

Much of Elberg's time was spent helping set trap lines and checking on them. He had no problem doing this; he expected as much knowing that the Cree were dependent on these animals for their survival. He volunteered to butcher a dead beaver and felt honored when given its forelegs as a thank-you.

Life was hard. With the temperature hovering at below 40 degrees Celsius, he often accompanied Bobby to check the fish, as well as the animal lines. Bobby's capacity to withstand the cold astonished him.

In the frigid air, Bobby stuck his bare hands under water, pulling out a bit of the net at a time, removing the fish one by one, and then putting the net back into the water.

"Aren't your hands frozen," Elberg inquired after an hour of continuous work.

"The water is warmer than the air, so it's not a problem," he answered.

The community, which consisted of about 700–800 people, was welcoming. It was also self-contained maintaining minimal contact with the outside world. There was only one radiotelephone; those who wanted to use it needed to go through an operator who connected them to another operator in Alma, Quebec who, in turn, connected them to a telephone line. Only one person could talk at a time, and anyone on the radio network could listen in on the conversation. Newspapers and radios were rare, and there were no televisions. Adding to the difficulties, the children attended the infamous residential schools run by missionaries out to expunge native culture.

Problems with alcoholism abounded. While there, Elberg befriended Walter, a pleasant, easy-going fifteen-year-old. Years later, while inebriated, Walter ran over two of his children while backing out of his driveway. Elberg doesn't know how much of this heavy drinking still goes on; many communities have since become dry zones and no longer allow alcohol into their communities.

The Inuit and Cree saw themselves then—and many still do so today—as living between two worlds: The assimilationist world of the missionaries—many Indians and Inuit became Christians—and the ways of their parents and ancestors, which appeared less relevant as modernity took hold. This dichotomy led to generational conflicts, as well as to a crisis of identity. In his 1984 paper, Elberg notes the following:

Younger Inuit are criticized by their elders for not being knowledgeable hunters, not knowing how to build a snow house, or not speaking the language properly. These youths listen to the words of the people they revere and feel ashamed, humiliated, inferior. They are told they are not real. This issue of "real Inuit" was raised by young Inuit (under forty) when I conducted fieldwork in a northern Quebec community in 1980–81. These people were astonished that I wanted to speak to them to conduct cultural research. Many told me, "It's usually the older people who get spoken to, who get asked the questions." They were hesitant, saying they were not used to talking about their way of life. One person, even though he was constantly sought by older people as a hunting companion because of his skills when I interviewed him about hunting, said that he "came a bit too late," because many of the skilled hunters had passed away. He was surprised that I talked to him, rather than a "real hunter, about that subject."

Moreover, the younger people, regardless of their chronological age, see themselves as five-years-old in Inuit time, as that was the age when they began attending the white man's schools and stopped learning Aboriginal ways.

Westerners, Elberg maintains, generally misunderstand Aboriginals, viewing them as culturally homogenous when nothing can be further from the truth. The West Coast Indians, for example, created sophisticated, advanced social organizations, while the Northern Quebec Cree maintained simpler social structures. "Pre-contact [with the white man] Native Americans were very much on the move. There was much warfare between them; these simple ideas that we like to project of a noble savage aren't true," he says.

Indians and the Eskimos constantly warred against each other. In the early days of the fur trade in the James Bay area, the Cree captured Eskimos as slaves. Mentalities have since changed. In one Hudson's Bay community, the Cree and Inuit lived apart from one another despite physically living side by side: today, they co-exist, and even pray together in a new, beautifully designed church.

Westerners also tend to patronize Aboriginals, believing that they are incapable of speaking for themselves, according to Elberg. However, there are many effective spokespeople, activists, lawyers, hunters, businesspeople, professionals and government ministers among them. Furthermore, we often place native people into slots of our own making. We see them either as victims and objects of our pity, as entertainment, or as spiritual masters who can teach us about mother earth and the environment, instead of just letting them be who they are.

These expectations infected way too many of them who ended up fulfilling the roles written for them. The Inuit, he says, are highly intelligent—you need to be very smart to survive those conditions—and yet tragically, far too few are given the opportunity to apply their innate intelligence in meaningful ways. Far too many Aboriginals, in general, live on transfer payments and make-work jobs created by the Federal government. There is, as well, rampant corruption, as heads of some communities often direct Federal monies and jobs to themselves and their families. "I hope they don't go down the path of perpetual victimhood. I hope they go the way of working with their abilities and strengths. With the James Bay Agreement, the Cree are now on that path; I hope they continue that way," Elberg states.

Machla Abramovitz
co-editor

Introduction

In 1968, Palestinian terrorists hijacked an El Al plane, and got away with it. They used the tactic repeatedly after that, with varying degrees of success. The most infamous incident was the forcing of Air France plane to Entebbe, Uganda, and Israel's successful rescue of the hostages.

More such rescue operations are required these days, but not of aircraft. The Palestinians and their Islamist allies have taken to hijacking peoples and causes. For example, in 1975, Betty Friedan, a feminist trailblazer, led the American delegation to an International Woman's Year World Conference. She was stunned by the conference's overt anti-Semitism and anti-Zionism. A 1980 Women's Conference in Copenhagen had a huge portrait of Iran's Ayatollah Khomeini, a man at the forefront of the oppression of women, decorating the conference chamber.

Furthermore, even though Israel is the only place in the Middle East that legally safeguards Gays from persecution, Toronto's annual gay pride parade has frequently featured the participation of "Queers Against Israeli Apartheid." That Gays would promote a movement that brutally oppresses them points to the effectiveness of Palestinian hijacking techniques.

The collection of articles in this publication examines the relation between Native American and Jewish issues, focusing on the perceived attempt to hijack the Native American struggle for rights and recognition into the framework of Palestinian suffering. Native Americans are viewed as the quintessential victims, having suffered genocide, theft of lands and consequent marginalization. Palestinians are similarly cast as victims of colonialism and oppression.

The hijacking doesn't just take place in protest marches and conferences. A Wisconsin Ojibwa Indian told me of her fear of the inroads Muslims have made in the local native communities, marrying Indian women and then using their new status to gain influence in native affairs and policies. An expert in Southwest Indian art claims that Lebanese, Syrian and Palestinian Arabs have been buying native art businesses in Arizona and New Mexico, then selling "Navajo" art made in the Philippines. When I asked him to write about this for our publication he refused, not even wanting his name mentioned. "People have been killed," he explained.

The left has long revered the oppression of native peoples and tried to make the most of it. Pretend Indians such as Ward Churchill and Elizabeth Warren used ostensible native identity to advance their careers. Steven Salaita, a minor academic who has written paeans glorifying Palestinian suffering was supposed to join the American Indian Studies program at the University of Illinois; his overt anti-Semitism got in the way.

Also getting in the way is that many Native Americans aren't interested in perpetually playing the victim. It doesn't fit their traditions or values. And while they may have been downtrodden in the past, they don't want that to define their future. They want to make their own lives.

The Navajo, for example, want to improve the efficiency of their agriculture. We provide a link in the bibliography on how the Navajo Nation is working with Israel to improve its expertise on efficient irrigation in an arid climate

Other Native Americans are businessmen, professionals. Many, both men and women, have served in the military, and cannot accept the reflexive anti-Americanism of the Palestinian agenda. Many are devout Christians, and cannot accept the Muslim agenda.

But more than that, they are themselves. Native Americans are not anybody else's stooge or weapon. The attention from the left may be enjoyable for a time, but ultimately it is another form of co-option, another form of exploitation. The Palestinians may claim that they are "indigenous," but as our contributors deftly show, there is no moral or historical equivalency with Native Americans.

Most popular opinion agrees that mankind has a common place of origin, whether in the Garden of Eden in some unknown location between the Tigris and Euphrates, or somewhere in Africa. If you go back far enough, everybody on earth has common indigenous roots.

It's when we start going only part way back that things get more complicated. Populations have never been stable. The Bible (cf. eg. 2Kings 17) tells us how the Assyrians displaced whole nations, replacing them with populations from elsewhere. If we prefer non-Biblical sources, speakers of the Turkic language group (Ottoman Empire) can be found far from their Turkish homeland, in China and Siberia, where they are now indigenous peoples.

Examples can be found in North America as well, such as the disappearance of the Tunnit (Dorset) peoples of the north, displaced by Inuit and Indians. The Cheyenne were pushed out of the Great Lakes area, in turn coming into conflict with other Native Americans and of course the U.S. Army. The Inuit battled the Ojibwa, Cree and Athabaskan Indians for territory. Warfare and population transfer happened both before and after the onset of European colonization. Are Native Americans indigenous to the specific places they now inhabit? A bigger question is "does this matter?"

If we adopt a synchronic criterion of indigenous status, that is, a definition at a specific point of time, then everyone and no one are indigenous. Whether we shout "1967," "1948," "1867" (Canada's independence from Britain), "1763" or "1492," we run into problems when indigenous status reflects a particular slice of time. This simplistic approach may be useful for sloganeering, but our contributors take a more sophisticated approach.

Ryan Bellerose and David Yeagley, each coming from opposing sides of the political spectrum, observe how Native American rights are an attractive issue used to legitimate other causes. Many movements have tried to appropriate or incorporate oppression of Native Americans into their own causes. As Margaret Atwood pointed out in *Survival*, her guide to Canadian literature, the Indians have become the quintessential victims, doomed to forever remain so. Jay Corwin uses a literary approach to negate the victim/ perpetrator narrative as it constrains both Native Americans and Jews, relegating them to a mythological realm. As characters in such a realm, both Jew-s, and Native Americans are condemned, unable to act to bring about their freedom. Perhaps the real sin of Israel in the eyes of the world's media is its refusal to abide by the rules of fantasy. According to this paradigm, Israel has no right to return fire when it's attacked. Fantasy characters don't carry real guns. Bellerose, Yeagley, and Corwin argue that refusing to be a victim doesn't make one an oppressor. The attempted appropriation of Native American issues is a form of exploitation.

In his "Conversation with an Indian friend," Bellerose lays out the misconceptions that facilitate lumping Israel and the Jews with the oppressors of Native Americans. Once that grouping is made, it's easier to build Native solidarity with other people who claim to be victims of the same oppressors.

Although Scott Benlevi "Walks Two Worlds," he has three names: Scott Benlevi, Walking Knife (English translation of his Shawnee name), and Shamir ben Togormah ben Avraham. He describes his tribal, family and personal histories, the former starting in the Ohio Valley, the latter ending up in Israel. There is no conflict between his Shawnee identity and dwelling in Israel. In a culture in which diversity is not necessarily a pejorative, it is possible to successfully walk both worlds.

Robinson discusses the ultimate expression of those misconceptions in his account of the Ahenakew affair. David Ahenakew was an important Native American leader, earning the Order of Canada for his achievements on their behalf. He was also a rabid anti-Semite, schooled in hatred in both Germany and Gaza. Ultimately stripped of the Order of Canada, his racism was denounced by other native leaders.

Ambassador Baker, in his article "The Indigenous Rights of the Jewish People," explains the significance of a people being indigenous, in terms of history, politics, and law. He uses this to examine concepts of legality and illegality of the presence of Jews in various parts of Israel, rejecting nomenclature that delegitimizes that presence.

Uqittuk Mark's connection to Israel is Biblical, rather than political. A devout Christian, he went on an organized Israel pilgrimage to see the land of the Bible. His attachment to the land transcends the politics, while his experience as an Inuk (Eskimo) gives him a clearer perspective to understand the struggles over it.

Mara Cohen has indigenous status in two worlds: as Lakota Indian and a Jew. Describing the potential of dual status as a source of conflict, she explains how it rather provides the ability to see reality through multiple perspectives and to move with ease between cultures.

Rabbi (Chacham) Jose Faur is an Argentinian-born scholar now living in Israel. He studied and taught at leading institutions, both rabbinic and academic. He also published many influential books and articles, touching on history, linguistics, Torah interpretation, and philosophy. His article "Jews, Conversos, and Native Americans: the Iberian Experience" is abridged from the original in the *Review of Rabbinic Judaism*.

Allen Z. Hertz was a senior advisor in the Privy Council Office serving Canada's Prime Minister and the federal cabinet, including with respect to aboriginal issues. He formerly worked in Canada's Foreign Affairs Department and earlier taught history and law at universities in New York, Montreal, Toronto and Hong Kong. His article "Aboriginal Rights of the Jewish People" emphasizes the companion aspects of the self-determination rights of the Jewish People and its millennial aboriginal rights in its ancestral homeland.

Sally F. Zerker is a Professor Emeritus at York University, where she began teaching in 1968 and was Director of Canadian Studies for a decade in the 1980s. A Toronto native and long-time resident, she received her Ph.D. in economics from the University of Toronto. Although her scholarly work focused on Canadian economic history, she has applied her expertise and insight to a wide range of material, including the political economy of the international oil industry. In 2017, CIJR published her open letter to the President of York University decrying the destructive effect of radical progressive ideologies on education. In this volume, her essay "Israeli 'Occupation': The BIG LIE" tears apart the polemics of those ideologies as applied to Israel.

The eightieth birthday of American Supreme Court Justice Louis

Brandeis was marked in a 1936 volume of the journal *Indians at Work* by John Collier, a Commissioner of Indian Affairs. Mara Cohen introduces the significance to Indians of Justice Brandeis.

Nathan Elberg spent a winter trapping with Cree Indians in northern Quebec. He writes how his hosts helped him understand a two-thousand-year-old Rabbinic teaching.

Finally, while Palestinians and their supporters work hard to appropriate Native American identity and victimhood, Howard Schwartz explains why the early European colonists were convinced that the native people they found in North America actually were Jews: descendants of the Ten Lost Tribes. Schwartz explains the ideology which led the colonists to interpret native culture as primitive Judaism, and then ultimately reject that interpretation when its implications became clear.

Nathan Elberg
co-editor

Aboriginal Rights of the Jewish People

Reconciling Subsequent Rights of the Newborn Palestinian People with Prior Rights of the Age-old Jewish People

Allen Z. Hertz

Introduction

This essay is not just about the specialized discipline called "public international law" but *appropriately* also about history and comparative law—including anthropology and elements drawn from natural, Common, Canadian, USA, Islamic, and Jewish law. This article does not aspire to be any exhaustive survey of the moral and legal claims of modern Israel as a sovereign country within the international States' system. Rather, emphasis here is on the companion and complementary aspects of the self-determination rights of the Jewish People and its millennial rights in its ancestral homeland. Throughout, the argument is that the age-old Jewish People possesses long-exercised aboriginal rights of entry, sojourn and settlement, which today extend at least from the Jordan River to the Mediterranean Sea. This paper thus dissents from United Nations Security Council Resolution 2334 of December 23, 2016, which egregiously erred in reaffirming "that the establishment by Israel of settlements in the Palestinian territory occupied since 1967, including East Jerusalem, has no legal validity and constitutes a flagrant violation under international law."

"Aboriginal" Versus "Indigenous"

The adjectives "aboriginal" and "indigenous" are commonly used for relative assessments that compare a couple of pertinent characteristics across populations:

> *First*, either term is more or less appropriately employed when the intention is to classify a local People as "domestic" relative to the "foreign" provenance or intrusion of one or more alien Peoples. By definition such a geographic comparison refers to at least two different places.

> *Second* are historical comparisons asking: *"Which one of the extant Peoples now in this country or region was here first in time?"* Referring to more or less the same geographic space, this is a temporal inquiry that includes at least three chronological periods—the present time plus the birthday or "date of entry" of each one of the *popular* contenders for the prize of local priority.

By both Latin etymology (*ab origine* = from the beginning) and English meaning, the word "aboriginal" specifically points to this key aspect of "being first" in the land. However, such explicit reference to priority is absent both in the English term "indigenous" and its Latin ancestor *indigenus*, the two of which equally mean "born in the land" rather than first in the land.

As between "aboriginal" and "indigenous," this semantic difference is not just a linguistic curiosity. Because priority can suggest a special connection to the land, being "first in time" has often been perceived as conferring prestige, legitimacy and sometimes rights. Among the extant local Peoples, who was there first can thus be of deep political interest. The identity of the true aboriginal People is understandably sometimes keenly contested. Priority in the land often features in ancient popular myths and also in millennial histories. However, there are also modern ethnic genealogies, including some newly fabricated with an eye to current disputes. With this "priority" issue so salient sociologically and politically, careful use of terminology is required to capture any distinction between an *aboriginal* and an *indigenous* People.

Consider extant Peoples in a modern country or region. First, in the land, the current aboriginal People may also be indigenous as they were literally born there. Alternatively, that current aboriginal People might have initially come from outside to an empty territory. And if not empty, any pre-existing populations might perhaps have been annihilated or assimilated. However, over the centuries, the land can gradually give birth (ethnogenesis) to one or more additional Peoples. If so, none of those later indigenous Peoples can ever be aboriginal relative to the current local People that was there first in time; just as that current aboriginal People retains its priority relative to Peoples subsequently arriving by conquest or settlement.

The one term "indigenous" has recently been promoted internationally in the *Declaration on the Rights of Indigenous Peoples* (2007). This Declaration provides no legal definition of "indigenous People." Itself disclaiming any pretension to be exhaustive, this UN instrument conceptually focuses, from an international perspective, on the domestic relationship between the current sovereign State and one or more indigenous Peoples. Notable is what the Declaration omits—specifically, it says very little about inter se relations among Indigenous Peoples and nothing at all about an "aboriginal" People.

What Are Aboriginal Rights?

The theme of "People" and "historic homeland" has for centuries resonated with Jews around the world. However, our own time sees an increasingly bitter controversy over the Jewish People's right to self-determination in all or part of its aboriginal homeland. That fierce debate inevitably involves the political and legal doctrine of the self-determination of Peoples. There is also the companion doctrine of aboriginal rights.

Legal systems frequently see long continued use, habit or custom as a source of law. For example, the English Common Law holds that the consistent practice of mooring a boat in a particular place can become a customary right after twelve to twenty years. Similarly, both anthropology and many of the world's legal systems recognize as group or tribal customary right, a rich variety of consistent collective practices dating back just a few decades, or maybe a century or two. For example, Canadian law acknowledges that, depending on particular circumstances, an aboriginal People can have distinctive "aboriginal" rights to both self-government and title to tribal lands. It is also possible for a tribe to enjoy aboriginal rights to specific practices like logging; hunting; fishing; crossing into Canada from the USA; and duty-free importation of goods for tribal use.

So, what of the more than twenty-six centuries during which *the great Jewish People of world history* famously kept some real demographic and cultural ties *in and with* its ancestral homeland? The answer was provided in May 1937 by then Jewish Agency Chairman David Ben-Gurion who astutely clarified that "the Jews coming to Palestine do not regard themselves as immigrants: they are returning as of right to their historic homeland." Ben-Gurion was juridically precise in then articulating "the right of Jews to enter Palestine and to re-establish there their National Home."

Ben-Gurion's reference to "National Home" pointed directly to relevant treaties which are the highest source of public international law. To the point—declarations, resolutions and treaties from the First World War and the subsequent peace settlement had already explicitly recognized the Jewish People's historic connection to its aboriginal homeland. And, half those treaties had specifically called for *facilitated* Jewish immigration and *"close settlement by Jews on the land"* everywhere west of the Jordan River.

Charles de Gaulle, president of the jaded, pragmatic and sometimes defeated country that was 20th-century France, quipped: "Treaties are like roses and pretty young women—they last as long as they last." But, don't expect de Gaulle's cynical, *Realpolitik* perspective on treaties to be shared by a beleaguered aboriginal People like the Jews. Pertinent experience in Canada, New Zealand and elsewhere shows that, if States recognize ancestral rights in a treaty with an aboriginal People, they can expect permanent reminders of that recognition and those rights. Precisely so is it written in the *Declaration on the Rights of Indigenous Peoples*; a document which characteristically highlights "the urgent need to respect and promote the rights of indigenous peoples affirmed in treaties." This is a powerful reminder that the Jewish People also has clear treaty rights that endure to this day.

In addition to such treaty rights, the Jewish People also has other kinds of rights as adumbrated in the 1948 *Declaration of the Establishment of the State of Israel*. There, the reference is to a "natural and historic right" to "the birthplace of the Jewish People," where "Jews strove in every successive generation to re-establish themselves." On December 2, 2012, the Israel Cabinet reaffirmed: "The Jewish People has a natural, historical and legal right to its homeland."

The concept of aboriginal rights has been well understood by other Peoples, e.g., by the Greek People in the 19th century when it fought for independence from the Ottoman Empire. Now speaking articulately about their aboriginal and treaty rights, the Indian tribes of Canada astutely perceive that *law is akin to an ongoing discussion about rights*, in which it is essential to offer meaningful arguments. That legal discussion is also a place where a small People tells its own story, which can be a compelling narrative that engages the conscience of others more powerful.

Napoleon's Proclamations to the Jews

Precisely such a reflection of gentile conscience were the one or more wartime proclamations which 29-year-old General Napoleon Bonaparte is alleged to have addressed to the Jewish People during his 1799 campaign in the Holy Land, which the French then included within their understanding of "Syria." Still harboring hopes that his army would soon conquer the whole Ottoman Mideast, Bonaparte is said to have then described "Israelites" as "lawful heirs" to their "ancestral land" and encouraged them to hasten home to reclaim their "patrimony."

News of Bonaparte's invitation to the Jews "to re-establish ancient Jerusalem" appeared in the Paris press on May 22 and 29, 1799. There were one or more similar reports in newspapers elsewhere in Europe. Whether from Paris and/or the Mideast, the story that Bonaparte had issued such a proclamation then rippled through Jewry stimulating ancient Messianic hopes.

Bonaparte's alleged initiative for the Jews had policy precedents. During the month before and after May 19, 1798, when Bonaparte's fleet sailed for Egypt, prominently published in Paris were some semi-official strategic points and propaganda about how France could richly gain by sponsoring the return of Jews to their ancestral homeland. This same calculation appeared in Bonaparte in Cairo or Memoirs of this General's

Campaign in Egypt. This was a rapidly written "current affairs" book rushed into print in Paris close to the end of 1798 or the start of 1799. Regarding restoration to the Jewish People (la nation juive) of "their land of origin," it was there argued: "The conqueror of Egypt is too good a judge of men to misunderstand the advantages which could be derived from this people in the execution of his vast plans."

Palestinians "a People" But Jews Not?

Denying or minimizing Jewish rights is an integral part of the ongoing war against the Jewish People and Israel. For example, both Palestinian leader Mahmoud Abbas and former Iranian President Mahmoud Ahmadinejad stubbornly deny that the Jews are a People, within the context of the modern political and legal doctrines of aboriginal rights and the self-determination of Peoples. Their persistent rejection of Jewish history and *peoplehood* is precisely the position earlier articulated in the 1964 Covenant of the Palestine Liberation Organization and the 1968 Palestinian National Charter:

> Judaism, being a religion, is not an independent nationality. Nor do Jews constitute a single People with an identity of its own; they are citizens of the states to which they belong.

Such denial of Jewish *peoplehood* is astonishing because an enormous body of archaeological and other historical evidence demonstrates that—like the Greeks and the Armenians—the Jewish People is among the oldest of the world's Peoples. Now, a quarter-century of genome research has produced a totally new kind of evidence suggesting that most of today's Jews are, to an appreciable extent, genetically interrelated and significantly descended from Jews of the ancient world.

Early sources establish that Mideast man understood the idea of *peoplehood*. For example, then self-identified "Jews" regarded *peoplehood* as one of the principal motors of world history, as shown in the biblical *Book of Genesis,* from perhaps around 600 BCE. Referring to a particular popular name and also to shared ancestry, territory, language and achievement, *Genesis* (in the story of the Tower of Babel and elsewhere) describes what it means to be a distinct People alongside other named Peoples from a sociological perspective.

Thus, the early modern European Peoples were much later able to derive their understanding of what it means to be *a People in history*, principally from the story of the Jewish People, as powerfully portrayed in the Hebrew Bible. That book, in its various translations, was one of the foundation stones of European civilization.

The Hebrew Bible also exercised considerable influence on the development of Islam. Thus, referring to the *Taurat* (Arabic: تَوْرَاة), the Koran endorses the Torah or Pentateuch (Five Books of Moses) as part of the revealed word of God. The Koran also tells the story of the Jewish People, including its special connection to the Holy Land.

What Is "a People"?

Linguists have theorized about whether there was ever a proto-Semitic language. This famous linguistic theory was eagerly *racialized* to suggest kinship among the alleged Semitic-speakers. If so, any such genetic connection would have to reach far back into prehistory and today awaits further findings from the new genome science.

From linguistics far more pertinent to the phenomenon of Jewish ethnogenesis are the immediate origins of the Hebrew language in the half millennium after 1500 BCE. Finally born around 1000 BCE was a particular tongue biblically known as the "language of Canaan"

(Hebrew: *sepat kena'an* שְׂפַת כְּנַעַן) or more frequently as "Jewish" (Hebrew: *Yehudit* יהודית).

The specifically "Hebrew" language (Hebrew: *ivrit* עברית) is not explicitly identified as such anywhere in the Bible. Using "Hebrew" as the name for the language of the Jews seems to have first occurred in the 2nd century BCE. At the dawn of the Common Era, the "Hebrew" language (Greek: *Hebraisti* Ἑβραϊστὶ) appears several times in the Christian gospels, where the reference probably points to Aramaic.

That bit of linguistic history is useful to teach that *peoplehood* is not just about genetics; but is rather simultaneously a complex sociological phenomenon—partly a conceptual artifact or symbol, always something of a cultural invention. Significantly analogous to the trademark of modern intellectual-property law is *the particular name* which a specific population commonly uses to consistently self-identify as a distinct People, as distinguished from other Peoples.

For example, consider in clear chronological order and specific historical context, the ethnonyms—יהודים Yehudim = Jews; 汉人 Hanren = Han People (i.e. the Han Chinese); українці Ukraïntsï = Ukrainians; and Québécois = Quebeckers. General self-identification under such a definite name is the key expression of group self-consciousness that simultaneously signals and enables collective political ambition.

Beyond its chosen popular name, the pertinent group must also share some relatively distinct social and cultural features drawn from a wide-open menu, potentially including ancestors, language, history, homeland, territory, rites, rituals, religion, mores, etiquette, laws, citizenship, institutions, mythology, folklore, writing system, literature, drama, painting, plastic arts, dress, diet, cuisine, dance, music, games, sports, agriculture, and economy. Thus, every People is not marked by the same set of shared characteristics. However, there is little difficulty in identifying a particular People and distinguishing one from another.

In addition to its *subjective* identity, such a specifically *named* People normally attracts a companion *objective* identity in the eyes of its friends and enemies, who from each succeeding century provide valuable historical evidence about its existence and characteristics. Critical is this reference to *subjective* and *objective* evidence from each successive period.

For example, compelling objective evidence comes from the early 7th-century BCE cuneiform inscriptions of the Neo-Assyrian King Sennacherib written in Standard Babylonian Akkadian. Reference there is to the defeat (701 BCE) of Hezekiah "the Jew" *(ia-u-da-a-a)* who was said to be king of a country called Judah *(ia-u-di):*

> As to Hezekiah, the Jew *(ia-u-da-a-a)*, he did not submit to my yoke, I laid siege to his strong cities, walled forts, and countless small villages, and conquered them by means of well-stamped earth-ramps and battering-rams ... Himself I made a prisoner in Jerusalem, his royal residence, like a bird in a cage.

Subjectively, the ethnonym *Yehudim* appears biblically numerous times in Hebrew and Aramaic. For example, in the *Second Book of Kings*, there are two separate references to *Yehudim* by way of contrast to Edomites and Chaldeans respectively. These early biblical references complement independent epigraphic sources referring to the polity *Yehuda* or the ethnonym *Yehudim*. For example, pertinent are famous stelae, royal seals of the Kingdom of Judah, and Neo-Assyrian and Neo-Babylonian cuneiform inscriptions. Combining such solid extra-biblical evidence with what we have long known from the Hebrew Bible allows us to conclude with a high degree of confidence that by 600 BCE there already existed a distinct population:

- *in/from* the kingdom of *Yehuda* (יְהוּדָה);
- using a language called *Yehudit* (יהודית); and
- self-identifying as *Yehudim* (יהודים).

Without exception, this *popular* name *Yehudim* can be validly translated into English as "Jews"—rather than as "Judahites" or "Judeans." Those last two English language variants—preferred for purely contextual or interpretative reasons—are entirely extrinsic to the precise ethnonym *Yehudim* as expressed in the original Hebrew, Aramaic or Akkadian.

Due to a complex historical rationale explained in the Bible, those Jews and their descendants down to this day have always retained for the specifically "Jewish" People—in addition to its *popular* name *Yehudim*—the companion rhetorical, poetic, high-register, liturgical, sacred name *"Israel"* (Hebrew: ישראל). This powerful *cultic* ethnonym appears in many biblical passages including the famous: *"Hear, O Israel!"* (Hebrew: *Shema Israel!* שמע ישראל) In mid-May 1948, parallel historical and linguistic considerations probably dictated the last-minute choice of "State of Israel" (Hebrew: *Medinat Israel* מדינת ישראל) as the official name for the new Jewish country.

Aboriginal by Genetics Alone?

Nazis, racists and racialists may dissent, but there is currently no authoritative political or legal doctrine of the *aboriginal rights of genes* or of the *self-determination of genes*. Rather, aboriginal and self-determination rights pertain to a culturally complex, sociological "People" born via general self-identification under a specific name, like "Jews" (Hebrew: *Yehudim* יהודים).

This factual reality explains why the modern political and legal idea of *peoplehood* is flexible enough to embrace the specifically "American" People, which is famously of mixed ancestry; and also the virtually homogeneous, self-identified "Japanese" People. Thus, *peoplehood* is available to the population of a nation-State like Croatia, with a very high percentage of common ancestry; but also to the population of Canada, a country for the most part recently settled by ethnically diverse migrants. There, common ancestry can be less salient, with the distinct "Canadian" People now more importantly self-defined by shared institutions, laws, citizenship and territory.

For profound practical reasons, historic or remixed populations sometimes opt to rebrand with new self-identifications that are always politically meaningful. Thus, a new *named* People emerges from time to time (e.g., the *Québécois*); while an older distinct People may significantly subdivide or disappear—in most cases, with genes and cultural characteristics partly persisting in populations of one or more other Peoples.

For example (as discussed in detail below), it was only in the period after the June 1967 Six-Day War that the great Arab People subdivided to give birth to a distinct "Palestinian" People. This specifically "Palestinian" People was born when a particular Arab population—*exactly as it was post 1967*—for the first time generally self-identified by referring to the toponym "Palestine." Such rebranding powerfully signaled politically; hardly a surprise given its connection with ethnogenesis, which is mostly a sociological phenomenon.

An existing People can today claim to be aboriginal either *in its own name* or perhaps by virtue of direct *succession* from an immediate parent People that had itself already claimed to be "the" aboriginal People there. However, a specific People cannot now suddenly claim to be aboriginal, solely by virtue of some recently alleged genetic descent from a culturally remote or unrelated ancient People with a different name.

Today turning to antiquity to make an aboriginal claim *in its own name*, a distinct modern People needs to show not only some credible genetic roots, but also a continuing socio-cultural identity that, without a break, reaches back across each century to the relevant historical time.

Logically and juridically, a current People cannot now make an aboriginal claim *in its name* concerning historical periods before its ethnogenesis, i.e., when the pertinent population did not yet generally self-identify as that particular People. Nor can a distinct, modern People's right to national self-determination now be claimed *in its name* to apply retroactively in a historical period before its ethnogenesis.

Which Is "the" Aboriginal People?

Among the distinct, self-identified Peoples *now* living in a country or region, the one with the best claim to be aboriginal is the specifically named People that was there first in time. Without reference to numbers, this *now existing* aboriginal People is distinguished from the other *current* local Peoples which subsequently either were formed in the land *(indigenous)* or came there via conquest, migration and settlement.

For example, 1860s British North America witnessed creation of a new country called "Canada." In this connection, the Fathers of Confederation intentionally crafted a new "political nationality" to unite several mostly settler populations with contrasting self-identifications, largely based on differences of language, religion and ancestry. But across the 20th century, Canada completed its own trajectory "from colony to nation." According to the Supreme Court of Canada, a new specifically *Canadian* People gradually emerged via a process of general self-identification. Because this ethnogenesis occurred at home, this nascent "Canadian People" *as such* is certainly indigenous to Canada.

Nonetheless, the North American Indian tribes there significantly remain the "First Nations." They are still among the *aboriginal* Peoples of Canada, though some Indian bands now number only a few hundred individuals. Nor can their special status as "first in time" be erased, because the subsequently born "Canadian" People is also indigenous or because the First Nations are now just a fraction of Canada's population.

Like the First Nations, the Jewish People for more than two millennia has always had the strongest claim to be *the* aboriginal People in its ancestral homeland—though for most of those centuries, Jews there were but a small percentage of the local inhabitants. Nor is this persistent Jewish claim to be *the* aboriginal People there now in any way weakened because:

- the majority of Jews have at various times lived elsewhere;
- Jews are now once again the local majority; and
- local Arabs after 1967 *generally* opted to rebrand with a new self-identification as the distinct "Palestinian" People—which *as such* is arguably indigenous, as so recently born mostly between the Jordan River and the Mediterranean Sea.

Redemption Through Return to the Land

Matters relating to entry, sojourn and settlement are keys to Judaism's understanding of history. This responds to God's biblical command to live in "the land of Israel" (Hebrew: *Eretz Israel* ארץ ישראל). Entry and settlement are crucial because Jewish religion/history subjectively focuses on repeated migrations back to the Promised Land as redemption of the Jewish People. First, there was the return to settle in the land after the biblical exodus from Egypt. Second, there came the Jewish People's return to *Eretz Israel* after the Babylonian exile in the 6th century BCE. Finally, throughout the Common Era, there is the prospect of the Jewish People's redemption to be effected by Jews persistently "ascending" (Hebrew: *aliyah* עֲלִיה) to settle in *Eretz Israel*. Thus, the essential truth is that most Judaism has been "Zionist" millennia before the late 19th-century birth of political Zionism as a secular movement.

As in the *Declaration on the Rights of Indigenous Peoples*, aboriginal rights characteristically feature access to and use of tribal lands, including sacred sites and holy places. In this vein, Jews have always claimed *(inter alia)* rights to visit and/or dwell in their ancestral homeland. And significantly, they have stubbornly done so for more than two thousand years. Across the centuries, some then self-identified "Jews" always lived in their aboriginal homeland; and some other Jews, whether from the Mideast or abroad, persistently perceived a duty and desire to join them there.

Diaspora Jewry Famously Linked to Its Homeland

During the Roman period when Jews were the local majority, several million Jews worldwide felt strong religious obligation to famously make steady, annual payments for the upkeep and ceremonies of the Second Temple in Jerusalem. Roman emperors repeatedly reaffirmed this then controversial right of Jews throughout the Empire to contribute to the Temple's expenses. Stubbornly sticking to their own lunar calendar, Jews from Egypt to Babylon watched for the mountain-top signal fires that for centuries relayed from the Temple authoritative news of the start of the new month (Hebrew: *rosh chodesh* ראש חודש). The Second Temple was also the focus from the Mediterranean lands and beyond widespread Jewish pilgrimage.

Jews were still the local majority for several centuries after the 70 CE destruction of the Second Temple. During this later Roman period, Jews from near and far continued pilgrimage, but now with more focus on some other sacred sites like the Tomb of the Patriarchs in Hebron. Far-flung Jewish communities of the Roman Empire joined synagogues elsewhere in offering yearly payments in pure gold (*aurum coronarium*) to support their religious leaders in Palestine, until the Jewish Patriarchate there was abolished in the early fifth century CE. Roman emperors also explicitly confirmed the sometimes contested right of the Jews to collect the *aurum coronarium* and send it to Palestine. This ancient practice and its imperial confirmation were key expression and recognition of "organized Jewry in the Roman Empire."

For around fifteen hundred years after the abolition of the Palestinian Patriarchate, Jewish communities around the world regularly contributed to the *halukka* (Hebrew: חלוקה), a fund to help pious and/or indigent Jews living in *Eretz Israel*. With respect to obligations of charity, Jewish law (Hebrew: *halacha* האלאכהא) exceptionally prioritized helping the poor Jews of *Eretz Israel* over indigent Jews in the diaspora. Similarly recognized for many centuries was individual and collective Jewish responsibility to locally give alms to support Jews traveling to *Eretz Israel,* whether for pilgrimage or settlement.

Religious Importance of Living in the Land

The enduring high authority of the *Mishneh Torah* (משנה תורה), which Moses Maimonides finished in Egypt around 1180 CE confirmed the fierce focus on the sacred homeland. Maimonides was a famous physician, philosopher, and rabbi. He was also twice State-appointed head (Arabic: *ra'is al-yahud* رأس اليهود) of all the Jewish communities of Saladin's new Ayyubid Sultanate which was then fighting the Crusaders in the Holy Land:

> Great sages would kiss the borders of *Eretz Yisrael*, kiss its stones, and roll in its dust. Similarly, Psalms 102:15 declares: 'Behold, your servants hold her stones dear and cherish her dust.' The Sages commented: Whoever dwells in *Eretz Yisrael* will have his sins forgiven as Isaiah 33:24 states: 'The inhabitant shall not say "I am sick." The people who dwell there shall be forgiven their sins.' Even one who walks four cubits there will merit the world to come and one who is buried there receives atonement...

Such rabbinic emphasis on living in *Eretz Israel* was just one side of the coin. On the other side of the coin, the sultan Saladin, early in his reign, confirmed the rights of communal autonomy which Mideast Jews had previously enjoyed under the Fatimids. In 1187 CE, Saladin conquered Jerusalem and three years later invited Jews to return to settle there. This invitation must have delighted Maimonides. During the preceding nine decades, the Crusaders had mostly excluded Jews from the two holy cities of Hebron and Jerusalem. After Saladin's 1190 invitation, Jerusalem once again attracted a significant Jewish population, including from as far away as France.

Judaism, the "Aboriginal" Faith

Across two millennia, there have been important reciprocal influences among Judaism, Christianity and Islam. However, the latter two faiths generally acknowledged some historical derivation from Judaism as *forerunner.* Especially during their respective periods of local rule, Christian and then Islamic political, cultural, and demographic connections to Jerusalem and the Holy Land usually came with some awareness that Judaism there was *first in time*. For example, the two later religions theologically understood that, like the Jews, they too revered the Lord God of Israel. The two later faiths also importantly validated the Jewish historical narrative in the Hebrew Bible, which had considerable influence on the development of first Christianity and then Islam.

Let us recapture attitudes as they were before crystallization of the modern political dispute over Jewish self-determination in the Holy Land. Especially during their respective periods of local rule, Christians and then Muslims for close to two thousand years were generally aware of a broader context, in which the Jewish People always had a special connection to the land of its birth. There, Jews were subject to permanent discrimination, periodic persecution, and episodic restriction. However, across the centuries, minority status there generally did not preclude *(inter alia)* Jewish entry, sojourn and settlement. Nor are rights to such *millennial aboriginal practices* now diminished, because today Jews are again the majority of the local population.

Aboriginal Versus Majority Rights

Aboriginal rights are not invariably minority rights; but, in a minority context, aboriginal rights significantly contrast with majority rights, and limit the right of the current majority to decide all matters without regard to the aboriginal minority. This factual reality reminds us that "majority rules" is not a universal moral, political or legal principle that invariably applies to all subject matter, under all circumstances, and at all times.

Abundant polemical references to historical demography suggest that retrospectively imagining something like a hypothetical majority vote in an earlier period is now often an unspoken premise underlying current judgments about the moral weight of history. If so, we should recall that "majority rules" is *by itself* a relatively narrow principle that is notably more procedural than substantive.

Thus, we can safely suppose that, since antiquity, there was never a time when a moral or natural-law right to (potentially) bar Jews from their aboriginal homeland could have been derived *simply* from a hypothetical majority vote. In every conceivable instance, there would also have to have been alleged some further compelling reason (e.g., self-defence) as a substantive moral or natural-law justification for then (potentially) precluding one or more of Jewish entry, sojourn and settlement. Also, regarding each particular historical case, the moral or natural-law cogency of any such substantive reason for then (potentially) barring Jews would today have to be carefully weighed within the specific equities of that particular time and space, to which that justification pertains.

This current requirement of contemporary and contextual fairness points to some strikingly different historical, geographical and demographic situations. Thus, for potential examination is specific local circumstances in the broader context of the whole world as it once was. But also to be considered is the immediate framework of, for example, the erstwhile Fatimid, Ayyubid, Mamluk, Ottoman or British Empires. And, in that last British case, careful account must be taken of Mandate Palestine, both east and west of the Jordan River (1922–1946). However, Transjordan (Eastern Palestine) also remains part of the moral and political equation, long after the June 1946 entry into force of the UK treaty that cut the Hashemite Kingdom of Transjordan from Mandate Palestine.

Nor logically can such a retrospective assessment of a possible moral or natural-law justification for then (potentially) barring Jews now refer anachronistically to the interests of a distinct "Palestinian" People for periods before 1967, when local Arabs did not yet *generally* self-identify as the distinct "Palestinian" People.

If you like, you can retrospectively test the morality and fairness of then cancelling age-old Jewish rights of entry and settlement with the example of the May 1939 UK White Paper which is discussed below.

"Majority Rules" Not Retroactive

Is it appropriate to now make judgments about the moral weight of history based consciously or unconsciously on the metaphor or fiction of a particular hypothetical majority vote that was factually never held in the past? The stark reality is that the majority principle is a democratic "decision rule" that a current polity uses to select among present alternatives. Needless to say, the dead cannot rise from the grave to vote today; nor can we now issue writs for holding a referendum in the past. Thus, we can apply "majority rules" right now in our own polity, but not to an earlier historical period and place where—for any number of important reasons—men and women had failed to apply it in their own time.

Furthermore, the logic that renders impossible the retroactive application of "majority rules" is significantly complemented by the related principle that it is today's majority that governs rather than that of yesterday. Even within a current and continuing polity, the practical acceptance of "majority rules" depends on the systemic requirement for elections from time to time. And, the same iterative context that makes it possible for the losing minority to peacefully accept temporary defeat also requires the supplementary rule that it is the present majority that now governs. Thus, the authority of past majorities is evanescent. They are "the snows of yesteryear" to borrow a phrase from famed French poet François Villon.

For these reasons, the majority principle *alone* cannot now confer rights on a current minority *solely* because it had once been the majority. For example, think about the UK Liberal Party. It was a giant in British politics in the late 19th and early 20th centuries, but is currently a negligible player. Does anybody now suggest that the great Liberal landslide victory in the UK General election of 1906 by itself suffices to confer rights on that political party today?

Furthermore, consider the USA urban landscape that is the 13th Congressional District of New York. This constituency has experienced substantial demographic change and arbitrarily shifting borders, just like the "Palestine" that was invented during the First World War. Including Harlem, the 13th Congressional District was majority Black American during the first part of the 20th century. However, today, 55 percent of the local population is Hispanic and only 27 percent Black American. Should Hispanics have been told to stay out of the neighborhood? With regard to the 13th District, would anyone now argue that the minority Black Americans still have rights flowing from the one circumstance that they had been the majority there before 1950?

In the same way, taken in isolation, the bare fact that one hundred years ago Arabs were the majority between the Mediterranean Sea and the Jordan River logically cannot *by itself* create or sustain any *current* political, moral or legal right; and, most certainly not against the aboriginal Jewish People, which is today once again the majority there.

"The Jewish Movement Not Imperialist"

As across the last two millennia, so today! The presence of self-identified "Jews" in their ancestral homeland has always been *legitimately* aboriginal, not an expression of colonialism or imperialism. Agreement on this aboriginal aspect emerges from two contrasting, early Arab responses to political Zionism.

Born in Jerusalem in 1829, Yusuf Ziya Pasha al-Khalidi was an urbane, polyglot intellectual. He had served as mayor of, and Ottoman parliamentary deputy for Jerusalem where Jews were once again the local majority. As a Muslim, an Arab, and a subject of the Ottoman sultan, he wrote (March 1, 1899) to the Chief Rabbi of France, Zadok Khan, a friendly letter strongly warning against political Zionism. Therein, Yusuf Pasha explicitly welcomed some Jewish immigration provided that the newcomers would become loyal Ottoman subjects. However, he emphasized that the current political, military, ethnic and religious realities in the Ottoman Empire made Zionism impossible. Nonetheless, Yusuf Pasha's letter portrayed Palestine as the ancestral land of the Jews and validated their historical claim to be aboriginal there:

> Qui peut contester les droits des Juifs sur la Palestine? Mon Dieu, historiquement c'est bien Votre pays! [Who can contest the rights of the Jews regarding Palestine? Good Lord, historically it is really your country!]

After the 1918 shattering of the Ottoman Empire, more positive to the practicability of political Zionism was the Hashemite Prince Feisal ibn Hussein who was pertinently the principal Arab delegate at the 1919 Paris Peace Conference. There, American Zionist representative Felix

Frankfurter received from Feisal a March 3, 1919 letter saying: "We will wish the Jews a most hearty welcome home." Explicitly referring to Zionism, Feisal therein acknowledged: "The Jewish movement is national and not imperialist."

The Aboriginal Home

Generally and locally, many Muslims and most Arabs stubbornly reject the legitimacy and permanence of Israel as "the" Jewish State, i.e. as the political expression of the self-determination of the Jewish People in a part of its larger aboriginal territory. That ancestral homeland stretched from the Mediterranean Sea to lands east of the Jordan River. For example, the Hebrew Bible tells us that the Twelve Tribes straddled the Jordan River. Also extending eastward across the Jordan River was the northern kingdom of ancient Israel and then later Hasmonean Judea.

Since antiquity, this country was known to Jews as "the land of Israel," in Hebrew, *Eretz Israel*. The enduring cultural idea of the Jewish People's relationship to that particular bounded territory was always subjectively—and often also objectively—a populair ingredient in Jewish peoplehood. The Jewish case is a classic example of the sociological truth that conceptually a home is way more than just a tangible house and a homeland much more than merely a measured stretch of the earth's surface.

Christianity adopts elements from Judaism; and Islam similarly draws from the two older monotheistic religions. For this reason, "the Holy Land" as later understood by Christians (Latin: *terra sancta*) and by most Muslims (Ottoman-Turkish: *arz-i mukaddes*) was geographically identical to the earlier Jewish concept of *Eretz Israel*.

What Was "Historic" Palestine?

The forcible deportation of some Philistines, coastal *Philistia* (Standard Babylonian Akkadian: *Pilištu)* features more than once in the early 7th-century BCE cuneiform inscriptions of the Neo-Assyrian King Sennacherib. Better known are the many references in the Hebrew Bible. For example, the *Book of Exodus* specifically refers both to the "Sea of the Philistines" (Hebrew: *Yam Pelishtim* ים פלשתים) and to the littoral "Land of the Philistines" (Hebrew: *Eretz Pelishtim*ארץ פלשתים). The first extant Greek references to "Palestine" come eight times from alleged eyewitness Herodotus who wrote perhaps around 430 BCE. Not inconsistent with the aforementioned earlier sources, Herodotus perhaps means a particular stretch of the Mediterranean coast between Phoenicia and Egypt.

Greek and Roman writers into the 1st century CE, with some exceptions, understood Palestine as just the seaside strip associated with the memory of the Aegean Philistines who disappeared before the 6th century BCE. However, such narrow geographical usage expanded around 135 CE, when the entire Roman Province of Judea was officially termed *"Palaestina"* to punish Jews for their periodic, stubborn revolts against imperial Rome.

This Roman administrative toponymy explains why "Palestine" came to mean the entire Holy Land for Christians, eventually including those speaking Arabic. Authoritative 19th-century Ottoman-Turkish dictionaries by Sir James Redhouse indicate that Mideast Christians referred to the biblical "land of promise" or "the Holy Land" as *Diyar Filistin*, meaning "lands of Palestine."

As a Christian synonym for the Holy Land, "Palestine" was for centuries just a bare historical reference—nothing more than a fond memory of the early 7th century CE, when *Palaestina* was still part of the Roman-Byzantine Empire, with Christianity as official faith. Thus, a visit there prompted Mark Twain to accurately observe (1869): "Palestine is no more of this work-day world. It is sacred to poetry and tradition—it is dream-land."

A remembered, but literally non-existent Palestine had for centuries been *imagined* on European and American maps as invariably including lands east of the Jordan River. Thus, the 1911 edition of the *Encyclopaedia Britannica* captured the correct historical and geographical understanding in specifying that the Jordan River separates "Western Palestine" from "Eastern Palestine," which extends as far as the beginning of the Arabian Desert. Moreover, every actual "Palestine" that has historically existed, from the end of the 4th century CE until June 1946, has always included part or all of the territory that is now the Hashemite Kingdom of Jordan.

Holy Land's Population Migratory?

Though Classical demography is a guessing game, Jews may have numbered several million in the early Roman Empire. For more than a century *before* the 70 CE destruction of the Second Temple, most Jews preferred living in various places around the Mediterranean and beyond, rather than in their aboriginal homeland. In *Eretz Israel*, Jews nonetheless remained the majority, perhaps into the 6th century CE. Though some Jews always preferred to stay in their aboriginal homeland, others were continually moving in and out—a migratory pattern that has endured to this day.

Nor should it be presumed that such a migratory pattern only pertained to local Jews. Across the centuries, other ethno-religious components (e.g., Muslim Arabs) were also significantly coming and going. Millennial mother-to-daughter continuity was not the exclusive demographic pattern in this Afro-Asian corridor. The last thousand years have seen total local population living there occasionally drop to remarkably low levels. Such rounds of radical depopulation were subsequently partly reversed by some indigenous growth. However, from time to time, there have also been repeated waves of fresh migrants drawn from various ethnoreligious groups, whether from adjacent regions or further afield.

For example, in the late 18th and early 19th centuries, regional rulers like Zahir al-Umar (Bedouin), Ahmet al-Jazzar (Bosnian), and Mehmet Ali (Albanian) invited farmers and other Muslim Arab migrants from Egypt and elsewhere to help repopulate the land. Also, there were always newcomers who arrived without authorization. For example, from the sixteenth to eighteenth centuries, Bedouin from neighboring regions significantly migrated to the Holy Land, where some became sedentary, as encouraged by the Ottomans.

The magisterial UK Peel Commission in 1937 said there was not much effective control of land frontiers which, during the interwar period, remained mostly open to undocumented immigration by Arabs. If true for most of the first half of the 20th century when various treaties had already delineated some State boundaries, how much truer for overland migrants in earlier periods when internationally the Holy Land had no land borders whatsoever!

During the last millennium, the minority demographic of then self-identified "Jews" probably followed a pattern that was roughly a scaled-down version of what was happening there generally. Thus, Jews too were coming and going, and some who left later returned. During tough times, Jews maintained their local presence partly "relay race" style, with newcomers taking the baton from long-time Jewish residents. However, whether stationary, entering or leaving, Jews always saw themselves as part of the distinct Jewish People with the strongest claim to be aboriginal there. And what is more, this stubborn Jewish self-perception was sometimes shared by non-Jews like Napoleon Bonaparte, Yusuf Ziya Pasha al-Khalidi, Arthur Balfour, David Lloyd George, Feisal ibn Hussein and Woodrow Wilson.

Always Jews in the Holy Land?

The Hebrew Bible, the Christian Gospels and the Muslim Koran all refer to the Jewish People and its connection to the Holy Land. Since antiquity, there has never been a time when *then* self-identified "Jews" were absent from the Holy Land. Even when Jewish numbers dropped to a low point, the Holy Land was still home to learned rabbis famous throughout the Jewish world. Across at least 2,600 years, the *then* self-identified, *specifically* "Jewish" People continuously kept the same subjective/objective identity that always famously included significant demographic and cultural links to its native land, *Eretz Israel*.

In the first five centuries of the Common Era, Jews were still the majority in Palestine where they played a key role in Jewish civilization, including completion of the *Jerusalem Talmud*. Rabbis there then thoroughly discussed the geographic limits of *Eretz Israel*, because some specific rules for Jewish religious practice only applied within the boundaries of the aboriginal homeland of the Jewish People.

Written in Hebrew characters are the thousands of medieval documents from the famous Cairo *Geniza*. These are among the contemporary historical sources that reveal much about Jewish life in the Holy Land, during the subsequent period stretching from the Muslim conquest in the fourth decade of the 7th century CE to the Crusader victory in 1099.

Deep religious attachment to ancestral homeland motivated the pilgrimage of 12th-century physician, philosopher and poet Yehuda

Halevy. He traveled from the Iberian Peninsula via Egypt, and died near Jerusalem in 1141. After specifying the uniqueness of *Eretz Israel* for the proper practice of Judaism, Yehuda wrote: "Jerusalem can only be rebuilt when Israel yearns for it to such an extent that they embrace her stones and dust."

During this period of the Crusaders and the Ayyubids, Acre was an important center for Holy Land Jews, about whom we learn from a variety of sources. For example, pertinent are many *Geniza* documents and also accounts by the 12th-century Jewish travelers Benjamin of Tudela and Rabbi Petachia of Ratisbon. Acre was then for a brief time the home of Moses Maimonides and later of Moses Nachmanides, two famous rabbis who encouraged Jews to live in *Eretz Israel* for profound religious reasons.

During the Mamluk period (1250–1516), Jerusalem was sometimes seat for a deputy to the Egypt-based Jewish prince or leader (Hebrew: נָגִיד *nagid*) who as *ra'is al-yahud* headed all the Jewish communities of the sultanate. Fifteenth-century Holy Land Jews also feature in the letters of Rabbi Obadiah ben Abraham Bertinoro and the travelogues of Christian pilgrims like Arnold van Harff, Martin Kabatnik and Felix Fabri. There were also always Jewish pilgrims, about whom a local Jewish guide (early 1480s) told Felix Fabri:

> The Jews pile up these stones to occupy a place beforehand, for they hope that erelong they will again inhabit the Holy Land; and therefore their pilgrims, who come from far countries, take places beforehand, in which places they hope that they shall dwell after the return.

More abundant are sources from the four Ottoman centuries ending in 1917–1918. For example, 16th-century doomsday registers (Ottoman-Turkish: *mufassal defterleri*) record the names of local Jewish tax-payers. Evidence also comes from documents like some late 18th-century account books of the Jerusalem Jewish community. With the 19th century, travel books, letters, and consular reports join a flood of other sources about local Jews who also told their personal stories. Though the number of Jews there grew absolutely, they were then still just a fraction of the total population which—including all the Muslims, Christians and Jews—notably remained astonishingly low; probably, very much lower than in the early Roman Empire.

Aboriginal Peoples Include Jews, Greeks and Armenians

Among several other aboriginal Peoples of the Ottoman Caliphate were the Jews, the Greeks and the Armenians. The age-old Jewish People is aboriginal to its ancestral homeland, *Eretz Israel*, in the same way that the storied Greek People is aboriginal to the Aegean region and the Armenian People has millennial rights in its historic lands. In the Mideast and Mediterranean, the continuous history of the Jews, Greeks and Armenians reaches back to antiquity.

Pertinently, these three ancient Peoples were already present before arrival from Central Asia of any of the Turkic Peoples; and obviously long before the 13th-century CE origins of the empire of the Ottoman Turks. By the time of the Ottoman conquest, each one of these aboriginal Peoples already had its specific cultural identity that was in all three cases thoroughly entwined with its own distinctive, ethnic religion.

Across *la longue durée*, these three aboriginal Peoples did not like each other. Nonetheless, Jews, Greeks and Armenians had longtime common experience as victims of the Muslim Turks, right up until the collapse of the Ottoman Empire at the end of the First World War. To the point, each one of these aboriginal Peoples famously ranked as a *historically-victimized* population in terms of the evolving human-rights methodologies that were emerging at a faster pace during and after the First World War. In that important human-rights context, a *historically-victimized People* is now understood to be normally entitled to: *firstly*, a sincere apology; *secondly*, significant reparation; and *thirdly*, extra vigilance lest there be renewed victimization whether by the same or other perpetrators.

In the early 19th century, some prominent personalities like the English poet Lord Byron enthusiastically championed the aboriginal rights of the Greek People. Partly for this reason, some of the European Powers intervened to help Greeks win their independence from the Ottoman Empire. In 1821 CE, when some Greeks began their revolt against the sultan, they were probably a minority of the population in the territory that is now modern Greece.

In the 19th and 20th centuries, Greek history has been partly about the hundreds of thousands of diaspora Greeks, who gradually migrated to their core ancestral homeland. For example, many returned to Greece as refugees after the First World War, when British Prime Minister David Lloyd George had unsuccessfully backed the aboriginal rights of the Greek People to the Anatolian littoral. There, large indigenous Greek communities like Smyrna (Izmir) persisted from antiquity until 1922, when they were savagely destroyed by the Muslim Turks who in 1915 had killed one and a half million Armenians.

The horrific atrocity that was the 1915 Armenian genocide shocked the conscience of the Western world, notably including the Christian sensibility of both Lloyd George and USA President Woodrow Wilson. Writing to Congress about the plight of the Christian Armenians, Wilson (1920) significantly described his fellow Americans as:

> the greatest of the Christian peoples [with] . . . an earnest desire to see Christian people everywhere succored in their time of suffering, and lifted from their abject subjection and distress and enabled to stand upon their feet and take their place among the free nations of the world.

The Armenian genocide was also an important part of the moral context in which the USA and the Allied Powers decided to recognize both the Armenian People's right to self-determination in its ancestral territory and the Jewish People's historic rights in the Holy Land. Until the 1917–1918 British conquest, the Holy Land was still part of the Ottoman Empire, which Woodrow Wilson reviled. As early as the 1912 presidential campaign, he had already pledged: "If ever I have the occasion to help in the restoration of the Jewish People to Palestine, I shall surely do so."

For Jews of the Holy Land, the First World War brought repression, persecution, starvation, deportation and flight. Their numbers there dropped sharply from around 85,000 in late 1914 to about 40,000 by the time of the Mudros Armistice (October 30, 1918). During the conflict, Jews fleeing Western Palestine and other Jews who stayed there were both able to receive some crucial help from the U.S. Navy, because the USA remained neutral relative to the Ottoman Empire.

Locally and internationally, it was then reasonably feared that Jews in the Holy Land might soon meet a grim fate like that of the hapless Armenians. The supreme Ottoman leader there, Ahmet Djemal Pasha was already infamous for his role in the 1915 Armenian genocide. In 1917, Djemal wanted to begin similar death marches to drive Jews out of Western Palestine. However, he was stopped by principal ally Germany, including Generals Erich von Falkenhayn and

Friedrich Kress von Kressenstein who were then serving the Ottomans as commanders on the Palestine Front.

Well informed about the perilous wartime situation of Jews there, President Wilson in June 1917 confided to American Zionist leader Rabbi Stephen S. Wise: "When the war will be ended, there are two lands that will never go back to the Mohammedan Apache. One is Christian Armenia and the other is Jewish Palestine."

Urgently in need of American wartime help, the UK government knew that it had to defer to USA power and preference. It was certainly no accident that the Balfour Declaration, promising best efforts to create "a national home for the Jewish People," was adopted (October 31, 1917) by the UK War Cabinet only after careful consultations with President Wilson.

Entirely consistent with the Balfour Declaration were Wilson's January 8, 1918 "Fourteen Points." Therein, he included the pertinent requirement: "Nationalities that are now under Turkish rule should be assured an undoubted security of life and an absolutely unmolested opportunity of autonomous development." Thinking both globally and locally, President Wilson perceptively understood that there was no contradiction between seeking to realize in Palestine the right to self-determination of *the great Jewish People of world history* and the companion fact that Jews were undeniably also one of the Mideast Peoples that had long suffered under Ottoman rule.

President Wilson's support for immediate Jewish rights of entry and settlement was clearly expressed in the instructions (January 21, 1919) for the USA delegation to the Paris Peace Conference. These significantly recommended:

> That the Jews be invited to return to Palestine and settle there, being assured by the Conference of all proper assistance in so

doing that may be consistent with the protection of the personal (especially the religious) and the property rights of the non-Jewish population, and being further assured that it will be the policy of the League of Nations to recognize Palestine as a Jewish State as soon as it is a Jewish State in fact. It is right that Palestine should become a Jewish State, if the Jews, being given the full opportunity, make it such. It was the cradle and home of their vital race, which has made large spiritual contributions to mankind and is the only land in which they can hope to find a home of their own; they being in this last respect unique among significant peoples.

Aboriginal Rights of the First Nations

Conceptually, the Jewish People is aboriginal to its ancestral homeland (ארץ ישראל) in the same way that the First Nations or Indian tribes are aboriginal to their ancestral lands in the Americas. The modern Jewish People claims both aboriginal and treaty rights in parts of its ancestral homeland. Aboriginal and treaty rights are also claimed by the Aboriginal Peoples of Canada, including the First Nations. They firmly believe that their sovereign rights to their tribal lands extend back to the beginning of time, i.e., long before the origins of European, international, and Canadian law. In the same way, the age-old Jewish People's claims in its ancestral homeland reach back to antiquity and thus antedate the post-Classical birth of both Europe and the Islamic civilization.

The Common-Law courts began recognizing aboriginal rights in the 19th century. From 1982, the rights of the Aboriginal Peoples of Canada have explicitly featured in Canada's *Constitution Act*. The Supreme Court of Canada has decided that, where a First Nation maintains demographic and cultural connections with the land, aboriginal rights can survive both sovereignty changes and the influx of a new majority population, resulting from foreign conquest. Dealing with claims of right on all sides, the Court seeks to juridically reconcile the subsequent rights of newcomers with the aboriginal rights of a First Nation.

Today, the concept of aboriginal rights is also an important topic in Australia, New Zealand and the United States, and is now receiving some more attention internationally. For example, pertinent to the millennial phenomenon of aboriginal rights is the *Declaration on the Rights of Indigenous Peoples*. For obvious political reasons, this UN instrument notably lacks a legal definition of "indigenous People." Also due to political sensitivities, international law has never been able to formulate an agreed legal definition of "a People" for the companion doctrine of the self-determination of Peoples.

Spot on is the comparison between the aboriginal rights of the Jewish People and those of the First Nations of the Americas. On either bank of the Jordan River, "the Jewish People" was the aboriginal tribe and "the Arab People" the interloping settler population, notably including major waves of Arab immigration in both the 19th and 20th centuries CE.

For more than two thousand years, Jews have stubbornly exercised their aboriginal rights of entry, sojourn and settlement. Thus, whether a thousand years ago or today, self-identified "Jews" returning to join other Jews in the Holy Land, are not like the 17th-century Pilgrim Fathers who built English settlements in America, where they had neither ancestors nor native kin. Nor is the Jewish People in its own aboriginal homeland ever to be compared with the Dutch Boers in South Africa or the French *colons* in Algeria.

Judaism's Focus on Sacred Homeland

The self-identified, specifically "Jewish" People, *under that same name*, has for more than two millennia continuously affirmed its historical and demographic connections to its ancestral homeland. Thus, Eretz Israel has for at least twenty-six centuries been a central element in the religion of Judaism. This territorial focus was described by British Foreign Secretary Arthur Balfour who had been UK Prime Minister (1902–1905). In 1919, he wrote:

> The position of the Jews is unique. For them race, religion and country are inter-related, as they are inter-related in the case of no other race, no other religion, and no other country on earth. In no other case are the believers in one of the greatest religions of the world to be found (speaking broadly) only among the members of a single small people; in the case of no other religion is its past development so intimately bound up with the long political history of a petty territory wedged in between States more powerful far than it could ever be...

From antiquity, most Judaism has been a Messianic religion, including specific reference to the homeland of the Jewish People. Authoritative for centuries as a restatement of the law is the late 12th-century *Mishneh Torah* (משנה תורה) of Maimonides. This holds that belief in the coming of the Messiah is one of the thirteen essential articles of Jewish faith. For centuries, Judaism has affirmed that the Messiah will: (i) be a descendant of David, King of Israel; (ii) gain sovereignty over Eretz Israel; (iii) gather world Jewry together there; (iv) rebuild the Temple in Jerusalem; (v) restore full Torah observance in Eretz Israel; and (vi) bring peace to the whole world.

Born in Spain at the end of the 12th century, Moses Nachmanides was an influential rabbi, philosopher, physician and kabbalist. Having migrated to the Holy Land, Nachmanides emphasized that God's biblical command to take possession of the Promised Land is directed to Jews of all generations, including the period of exile. Nachmanides strongly concurred with earlier Rabbis who had assessed that "dwelling in the Land of Israel outweighs all the commandments."

Today, Jewish law (Hebrew: *halacha* האלאכהא) is the world's oldest continuously-functioning legal system. Jewish law has always explicitly recognized the Jewish People's legal rights in its aboriginal homeland, the precise boundaries of which were carefully defined by rabbinic discussion across the first three centuries of the Common Era. Make no mistake, more than two thousand years of *halacha* insist that the age-old Jewish People *at the very least* has ancestral rights of entry, sojourn and settlement in *Eretz Israel*.

How should we approach this longstanding phenomenon? One of the options is comparative law; namely, to look at the role that history and civilization play in the aboriginal case law of the Supreme Court of Canada. There, in a purely secular context, a range of anthropological data—like Judaism's persistent emphasis on God's gift of Eretz Israel to Abraham and his descendants—would likely be seen as historical evidence of the continuing importance of that particular land in the distinct culture of that specific tribe, i.e., the Jewish People.

Jews Are "the" Aboriginal People

Of all extant Peoples, Jews have the strongest claim to be *the* aboriginal People of the Holy Land *(Eretz Israel)*. There, the Hebrew language (Biblical Hebrew: יהודית *Yehudit*) and the religion of Judaism gradually emerged, leading to the birth of a *then* self-identified, *specifically*

"Jewish" People at least 2,600 years ago. Before then, the Holy Land was home, *inter alia,* to the immediate ancestors of the Jewish People, including personalities like Kings Saul, David and Solomon, famous from the Hebrew Bible.

Still earlier or at the same time, the Holy Land was also home to other Peoples—like the Philistines, Phoenicians, Ammonites, Moabites, Edomites, and Samaritans. However, with the sole exception of the few surviving Samaritans, all of those other ancient Peoples have long since vanished from the world. Nobody today is entitled to make new claims on their behalf, including by reason of a supposed genetic descent that is only recently alleged and without sound basis in history and genome science.

What then of that *dramatis persona* of world history known as "the Arab People"? As such, the great Arab People is aboriginal to Arabia, not the Holy Land. The religion of Judaism, the Hebrew language, and a *then* self-identified, *specifically* "Jewish" People had already been established in the Holy Land for about a thousand years before the 6th-7th century CE ethnogenesis in Arabia of the great Arab People— the birth of which was approximately coeval with the emergence of Islam and Classical Arabic.

Nor traditionally did the great Arab People of world history claim to be aboriginal to the Holy Land. Like Yusuf Ziya Pasha al-Khalidi and Prince Feisal, erudite Arabs always knew from the Koran that Allah had promised the Holy Land to the Jews, all of whom would return there by Judgment Day. Such Arabs were also keenly aware of their proud and persistent narrative that celebrated the heroic Muslim conquest of a Byzantine province then already inhabited by Jews, Samaritans, and Greeks.

From the initial Muslim conquest of the Holy Land in the fourth decade of the 7th century CE, Jews there suffered persistent discrimination and periodic persecution. However, neither the Arab People nor subsequent invaders succeeded in eradicating the local Jewish population or bringing an end to the enduring links between the great Jewish People and its aboriginal homeland.

To the contrary, for fourteen hundred years, then self-identified "Jews" continued to stubbornly exercise their millennial rights of entry, sojourn and settlement—and, even more so after the mid-19th century. For example, Jews *legitimately*, once again, became the majority of the population in Jerusalem from the 1860s. Across the 20th and 21st centuries, Jews still continue to exercise their enduring aboriginal rights of entry, sojourn and settlement. Thus, in the same way, Jews today are, once again, *legitimately* the majority between the Jordan River and the Mediterranean Sea.

This majority status means that the Jewish People can now draw some steadily increasing benefit from the key doctrine of the self-determination of Peoples, which normally allocates territory by the national character of the *current* local population. At the same time, the Jewish People also continues to affirm aboriginal rights in parts of its ancestral homeland. And, it will be seen that these Jewish aboriginal rights still have some political and legal significance in the ongoing dispute caused by the stubborn refusal of many Muslims and most Arabs to recognize the legitimacy and permanence of Israel as the Jewish State.

The Jewish State

Most Jews round the world see Israel as *the* Jewish State, i.e., as the political expression of the self-determination of the age-old Jewish People in a part of its larger ancestral homeland. Like other Peoples, the Jewish People has a right to self-determination. Though the self-determination of the great Arab People is expressed via twenty-one

Arab countries, Israel is the sole expression of the self-determination of the great Jewish People.

Some Western thinkers are now uncomfortable with the idea of a nation-State as the homeland of a particular *historical* People, i.e., a well-known *People in history*. If so, there is no special reason to target Israel, because other jurisdictions are also nation-States—for example, the Canadian Province of Quebec, Japan, Greece, and the countries of the Arab League.

In theory and practice, the "nation-State" model does not have to conflict with fundamental civil and human rights for aliens or for citizens who do not ethnically self-identify as members of the historical People that constitutes the majority. Moreover, the nation-State can also accommodate collective rights for one or more minority Peoples. Moreover, concerning such individual and collective rights, Israel domestic law is comparable to what is provided by other legal systems, and superior to what is offered in other countries of the Mideast.

Israel Born of the Ottoman Empire

Until the end of the First World War, the Holy Land was part of the Ottoman Empire. Thus, Israel and around two dozen other modern countries are in whole or in part successor States of the Ottoman Caliphate, which for four hundred years (1516–1918) was the principal Power in the Mideast. Apart from the ruling Turks, the Ottoman Empire was home to many other Peoples including Albanians, Vlachs, Greeks, Slavs, Copts, Armenians, Maronites, Alawis, Druze, Kurds, Circassians, Arabs and Jews.

For centuries, these Jews lived in a variety of Ottoman venues including Buda, Belgrade, Bucharest, Sarajevo, Edirne, Salonika, Constantinople, Bursa, Izmir, Aleppo, Damascus, Mosul, Baghdad, Basra,

Cairo, Alexandria, Tiberias, Hebron, Safed, Jaffa, Gaza and Jerusalem.

In November 1914, the Ottoman Empire opted to enter the First World War to fight against the UK and its Allies. As the fortunes of war began to favor the British Army, the UK government addressed the question of what to do with the multi-national Ottoman lands, both in the light of current British interests and the 19th-century liberal doctrine of the self-determination of Peoples. In this regard, the father of modern political Zionism, Theodor Herzl, in his 1896 manifesto *The Jewish State*, had already proclaimed that Jews, though living in many different places around the globe, constitute *one People* for the purpose of self-determination.

Why the Balfour Declaration?

The British decision to offer "best endeavours" toward establishing a national home for the Jewish People in Palestine had three principal motives:

Firstly, Palestine was key protection for the eastern flank of the Suez Canal, the crucial gateway to British India. UK strategic thinkers valued Zionism partly as a humanitarian pretext to justify their plans for longtime British rule in Palestine, which otherwise would have been claimed by France. Also known to the British was that President Wilson, absent Zionist cover, would have resented UK retention of Palestine as just another imperialist land grab.

Secondly, a more urgent and immediate British goal was generating enthusiasm for the war effort among several million Jews in Russia. After the March 1917 revolution that toppled Czar Nicholas II, Russia continued to be war weary and was known to be ready to abandon the Allied cause. The UK War Cabinet approved the Balfour Declaration just one week before Lenin's antiwar Bolsheviks seized power.

Thirdly, a longer-term target was facilitating migration and settlement to gradually realize the Jewish People's self-determination in its ancestral homeland. This last aim was explained by Foreign Secretary Arthur Balfour, as recorded in the minutes of the War Cabinet's (October 31, 1917) deliberations:

> There were considerable differences of opinion among experts regarding the possibility of the settlement of any large population in Palestine, but he was informed that, if Palestine were scientifically developed, a very much larger population could be sustained than had existed during the period of Turkish misrule. As to the meaning of the words "national home," to which the Zionists attach so much importance, he understood it to mean some form of British, American, or other protectorate, under which full facilities would be given to the Jews to work out their own salvation and to build up, by means of education, agriculture, and industry, a real centre of national culture and focus of national life. It did not necessarily involve the early establishment of an independent Jewish State, which was a matter for gradual development in accordance with the ordinary laws of political evolution.

The pertinent UK government declaration was communicated to Anglo-Jewry leader Lord Rothschild in a letter which was published on November 9, 1917.

A "Palestinian" People in 1919?

As Great Britain worked to defeat the Ottoman Turks, the world also began to learn about the national claims of the great Arab People.

Here recall the wartime exploits of Lawrence of Arabia and Prince Feisal, both of whom were present at the 1919 Paris Peace Conference, where delegates shown a powerful searchlight on the doctrine of the self-determination of Peoples, including the claims of the great Arab People.

However, nobody in Paris knew anything about a distinct Palestinian People. Had there then been such a specifically "Palestinian" People, its existence would certainly have been known to Prince Feisal, USA President Woodrow Wilson, France's Prime Minister Georges Clemenceau, British Prime Minister David Lloyd George and to the other leaders who came to work on the peace treaties.

Extensive local testimony and petitions collected in 1919 by the USA King-Crane Commission confirmed this assessment. Contrary to President Wilson's personal Zionist inclinations own Zionist inclinations, the Commission's procedure and conclusions were tilted toward Christians and Arabs and strongly against Mideast pretensions of the Jews. Thus, the Commission's report stressed that, in the Holy Land, both Muslim Arabs and Arabic-speaking Christians vigorously rejected the plan to create a new country called "Palestine" which they perceived to be part of the detested Zionist project.

Ever a Muslim State Called Palestine?

In 1919–1920, most local Muslim Arabs and Arabic-speaking Christians backed then current Arab plans to create a large Arab State with its capital in Damascus. They expected this new Arab country to include at least all of historic or greater Syria—namely what are today Syria, Lebanon, Jordan, Israel, Gaza, and the West Bank (Judea and Samaria).

For Muslims in the Holy Land, this broader geographic focus of self-identification was natural, because a large province of Damascus (Ottoman-Turkish: *Şam*) had at various times featured prominently in Muslim and Ottoman history. By contrast, the Ottoman Empire never had a province or sub-provincial unit called, or co-extensive with "Palestine," no matter how conceived. Nor had Muslim history ever known a *State* or a *province* called "Palestine."

After the Muslim conquest in the fourth decade of the 7th century CE, the Caliphate for a time kept the old Roman and Byzantine toponym *Palaestina*, arabicized as *Filistin*, for one district or *jund* of the province of Damascus. Straddling the Jordan River, this medieval *Jund Filistin* covered terrain that was just a part of the much larger Palestine that was:

- previously a province of the Roman-Byzantine Empire;
- then for centuries *remembered* by Christians everywhere; and
- finally *realized* again in 1922 as the League of Nations Palestine Mandate.

Global Self-determination Exercise

- The Paris Peace Conference was concerned with the task of accommodating the political interests of the victorious Allied and Associated Powers with the claims to self-determination of then *well-known* Peoples with long histories of self-affirmation and bitter suffering under foreign oppression. Thus, considered were difficult and entangled issues touching the self-determination of then already *famous* Peoples such as the Chinese, the French, the Germans, the Poles, the Finns, the Letts, the Estonians, the Lithuanians, the Czechs, the Slovaks, the Slovenes, the Croats, the Serbs, the Italians, the Hungarians, the Romanians, the

Bulgarians, the Greeks, the Turks, the Kurds, the Armenians, the Arabs, and the Jews.
- In this larger context, just one decision among many was creation of "a national home for the Jewish People." And, it is noteworthy that "national home for the Jewish People" was the exact phrase reiterated from 1917 to 1922, in a series of consistent declarations, resolutions and treaties that were ex post facto blessed by the 1923 Lausanne Treaty with the Turkish Republic, as successor to the Ottoman Empire.

Why a National Home for the Jewish People?

The explicit purpose was to implement the 1917 Balfour Declaration which "always meant an eventual Jewish State." This authoritative assessment was specified by then Prime Minister David Lloyd George and former Foreign Secretary Arthur Balfour to Colonial Secretary Winston Churchill in July 1921.

"Palestine" was then a non-existent country of uncertain extent that was described by the League of Nations in 1922 as "the Palestine Mandate." This was an entirely new British jurisdiction then expected to endure for a very long time. In addition to Western Palestine as the national home for the Jewish People, the Mandate also included Transjordan (Eastern Palestine), where in 1921; the British had acknowledged the presence of the Hashemite Prince Abdullah ibn Hussein, who was Prince Feisal's older brother.

The "national home for the Jewish People" was launched by the *Palestine Mandate of the League of Nations*. This international instrument specifically referred to "putting into effect" the Balfour Declaration as endorsed by agreement of the Principal Allied Powers at the San Remo Conference, April 1920. Drafted by the UK government, the *Palestine*

Mandate was unanimously adopted by the League Council (July 24, 1922), then consisting of Belgium, Brazil, China, France, Great Britain, Italy, Japan and Spain.

The *Palestine Mandate* was duly enacted under clear authority to explicitly define Mandate terms, specifically conferred on the League Council by the 1919 *Covenant of the League of Nations*. The *Palestine Mandate* was, therefore, legally binding at the very least on all League members. The *Palestine Mandate* was thus akin to a multilateral treaty that created international obligations and rights, as confirmed by the interwar Permanent Court of International Justice. The instrument's principal beneficiary was the Jewish People. According to the 21st-century International Court of Justice, the *Palestine Mandate* still has some important legal effects today.

The *Palestine Mandate* importantly also became a bilateral agreement, because verbatim repeated as the text of the *1924 Anglo-American Treaty*, which was ratified by the USA Senate. Thus, the USA most solemnly "consented" to all the terms of the *Palestine Mandate*. This was needed because the USA had never been at war with the Ottoman Empire, did not attend the San Remo Conference, and was not a member of the League of Nations. Summarizing USA obligations for the Secretary of State, Director for Near Eastern and African Affairs Loy W. Henderson (July 7, 1947) reported: "This Government has taken the position that the Mandate for Palestine, which incorporates the substance of the Balfour Declaration, is recognized by us as an international commitment."

The regime of the *Palestine Mandate* was unique *(sui generis)* in terms and purpose. Supervising the conduct of the UK as the authorized mandatory Power, the Permanent Mandates Commission of the League of Nations repeatedly refused to use generalizations about the postwar Mandates conceived as a system, if such systemic deductions were inconsistent with the specific terms of the *Palestine*

Mandate. By contrast, opponents of the national home for the Jewish People have (into the 21st century) tried to evade detailed terms of the *Palestine Mandate*, which they have sought to ignore, reinterpret or invalidate, including with reference to flawed understandings of general provisions in the *Covenant of the League of Nations*.

Well informed about the Holy Land, the 1917–1922 decision-makers knew the territory there to be significantly under-developed and under-populated. They also understood that the national home for the Jewish People would initially lack a Jewish majority population. There was a conscious choice to refer not just to the small number of Jews living locally, but also to the past, present, and future of the great Jewish People encompassing fourteen million Jews worldwide, including the one million then living in the Mideast.

The international decision to create a national home for the Jewish People was made not so much on the basis of local demographics, but explicitly due to "the historical connection of the Jewish People with Palestine." This was clear recognition of the great Jewish People's long affirmed and continuous links to its aboriginal homeland.

The *Palestine Mandate* also contained detailed stipulations requiring development of the national home for the Jewish People. Included were provisions calling for *facilitated* Jewish immigration and "close settlement by Jews on the land," from the Mediterranean Sea to the Jordan River (Western Palestine). Thus, this part of the global arrangements, after the First World War, forthrightly focused on millennial Jewish rights of entry and settlement.

Equity: Did Arabs Deserve All the Mideast?

After the First World War, failure to create a national home for the Jewish People in Western Palestine would have meant giving the great Arab People almost the whole of the Mideast inheritance; while denying the great Jewish People any share in the partition of the multi-national Ottoman Empire, where Jews had lived for centuries, including in the Holy Land.

Without doubt such an unfair result would have been unacceptable to David Lloyd George, Woodrow Wilson and their peers. Remarkably, they broke with centuries of antisemitism by then refusing to discriminate against the Jewish People. Within the global context of a worldwide peace settlement, *they equitably perceived the claim to national self-determination of the great Jewish People to be as compelling as that of the great Arab People.*

Those decision-makers strongly insisted that they had also done justice to the claims of the great Arab People which they believed they had freed from four hundred years of Turkish rule and helped on the road to independence via creation or recognition of several new Arab States on lands that had formerly been subject to the Ottoman sultan. For example, 77 percent of the territory of the Palestine Mandate was Transjordan (Eastern Palestine) which became an independent Arab State in June 1946.

With an eye to the Mideast and Western Palestine, exactly these "ethical issues" were described by Albert Einstein in a June 13, 1947 letter to Jawaharlal Nehru, shortly before the latter became nascent India's first Prime Minister:

> At the close of World War I, 99 percent of the vast, underpopulated territories liberated from the Turks by the Allies were set aside for the national aspirations of the Arabs. Five independent Arab states have since been established in these territories. Only one percent was reserved for the Jewish people in the land of their origin. The decision which led to the proclamation

of the Balfour Declaration was not arbitrary, nor the choice of territory capricious. It took into account the needs and aspirations of both Arab and Jew; and certainly, the lion's share did not fall to the Jews. In the august scales of justice, which weigh need against need, there is no doubt as to whose is heavier. The "small notch" in the land of their fathers, granted the Jewish people, somewhat redresses the balance.

1938–1939: Jewish Refugee Crisis

The world was already awash with Jews fleeing Germany and Austria, an international tragedy that prompted the fruitless Evian Conference of July 1938. In October 1938, the Jew-persecuting Nazis moved on into parts of Czechoslovakia. Subsequently, the situation for Jews got even worse due to the State-sponsored terrorism that was the November 1938 *Kristallnacht* pogrom across Germany, Austria and the formerly Czech Sudetenland. Then, the Nazis were doing their best to grab Jewish personal property and transform Jews into impoverished refugees. Every nook and cranny from Shanghai to the Dominican Republic was then frantically tested as hundreds of thousands of Jews desperately sought shelter from persecution. However, from the late 1930s, the British secret intelligence service MI6 worked actively in several European countries to impede Jewish attempts to escape Europe.

Concerning the Jews and the "national home for the Jewish People" in Western Palestine, the troubling story of King George VI is worth telling because it accurately reflects the general tenor of *official* British attitudes during his reign (1936–1952). Morally pertinent is the key circumstance that George VI was then King-Emperor over about one quarter of the globe's land surface, notably including many *sparsely-populated* territories—for example, Palestine both east and west of the Jordan River. But, during the 1930s, the King had little or no sympathy either for the national hopes of the Jewish People in Western Palestine or for the plight of Jewish refugees fleeing Nazi discrimination, oppression and persecution. Royal Private Secretary from 1943 to 1953, Sir Alan Lascelles later reflected that the King had stubbornly focused on two priorities: firstly, "how to beat the Germans"; and secondly, "how to retard the impending disintegration of the British Empire."

With regard to the national home for the Jewish People: Like his immediate predecessors, King George VI believed that the sovereign had special responsibilities with respect to British foreign relations. Thus, Buckingham Palace typically hosted (October 22, 1937) Sir Miles Lampson, the British High Commissioner and Ambassador to Egypt. Then disparaging UK treaty commitments pertaining to the Jewish People, the King all too breezily volunteered: "Old Balfour was a silly old man; and had given (or promised to others) something already belonging to someone else!"

That same 1937 sentiment foreshadowed the way George VI sought to exercise his perceived role in foreign affairs in late July 1945. Then, the King successfully dissuaded incoming Labour Party Prime Minister Clement Attlee from proposing the appointment as Foreign Secretary of Hugh Dalton who had publicly championed the moral right of Jews to migrate to Palestine. Dalton's strong Zionist stand dovetailed with the Labour Party's Palestine position for the 1945 general election. But, the King confided to Attlee a marked royal preference for Ernest Bevin as Foreign Secretary. Thus, Dalton became Chancellor of the Exchequer and Bevin got the Foreign Office. There, Bevin showed himself (as indicated below) to be exceptionally cold to the plight of Holocaust survivors and other Jewish refugees. Bevin was also a surprisingly energetic and dogged opponent of Jewish migration to Western Palestine. Long after Bevin's disdain for both Jews and Zionism became clear, he was still the Labour Party Cabinet Minister that the King preferred.

With regard to Jewish refugees: In late February 1939, King George heard from Chief of the Imperial General Staff Lord Gort that "a number of Jewish refugees from different countries were surreptitiously getting into Palestine." This news sparked an otherwise constitutional monarch toward executive action of his own. What did the King then choose to do? He did not turn to the First Lord of the Admiralty and to the Colonial Secretary to urge increased vigilance at sea and at overland entry points into Palestine. Instead, George VI was all the more blameworthy in asking his Private Secretary Alexander Hardinge to contact the King's close friend Lord Halifax, then Foreign Secretary. Perhaps this explains why on March 2, 1939, the Foreign Office telegraphed the British Embassy in Berlin:

> There is a large, irregular movement from Germany of Jewish refugees who, as a rule, set out without visas or any arrangements for their reception, and they attempt to land in any territory that seems to present the slightest possibility of receiving them. This is a cause of great embarrassment to His Majesty's Government.

Was this message to Berlin the result of the King's desire that the Nazis be encouraged "to check the unauthorised emigration" of Jews from Hitler's Reich? By the time that George VI took his reprehensible initiative, he likely knew that British representatives in Romania and other European countries had already started asking local governments and shipping agencies to help stop the flow of Jewish refugees who were being watched by MI6. With an astonishing lack of moral sense and compassion, King George had been "glad to think that steps are being taken to prevent these people leaving their country of origin."

Taken together, the King's words about Lord Balfour and Jewish refugees ironically constitute testimony proving that George VI actually believed: *firstly*, that the UK had indeed promised Western Palestine to the Jewish People; and *secondly*, that there really was a logical connection between those two arguably separate topics of "Palestine" on the one hand and "Jewish refugees fleeing Germany" on the other.

The Nazis did not finally prohibit Jewish emigration from the Reich and from the German-occupied territories until the second half of 1941, a fact little appreciated. Before that time, many more Jews would probably have escaped from Europe but for the fact that they really had nowhere else to go. In this regard, King George VI and his government were particularly culpable, because—all things considered—internationally they then played the most prominent part in blocking the departure of Jewish refugees from Europe.

Jewish Rights Erased by 1939 UK White Paper?

Released on May 17, 1939 was the statement: "After . . . five years, no further Jewish immigration will be permitted unless the Arabs of Palestine are prepared to acquiesce in it." This prohibition was the crux of a British government White Paper entitled *Palestine: Statement of Policy*. Also promised was "establishment within ten years of an independent Palestine State." This radically new direction was driven by the 1936–1939 revolt of the Arabs of Palestine and also by sense of impending war with Germany.

In addition, the White Paper was significantly a product of enduring British belief in Pan-Arab nationalism. This was a 20th-century ideology that the British had themselves sponsored during the First

World War as propaganda to help defeat the Ottoman Turks. But more often than not, the British themselves genuinely believed in the existence and rights of *the great Arab People of world history*. This particular UK perspective partly explains why the White Paper was discreetly negotiated, not with the leaders of the Arab rebellion in Palestine, but rather with the neighboring Arab countries, i.e., with the British protégé Prince Abdullah (Transjordan) and the newly independent Arab States of Iraq, Egypt and Saudi Arabia.

Some members of the Permanent Mandates Commission thought those foreign governments had no right to interfere in Palestine. Nonetheless, the UK Cabinet was by April 1939 hell-bent to make a deal with "the Arabs" writ large. Specifically, the British hoped that pleasing the Arab States with regard to Palestine might be an effective way: *firstly*, to win the support of the Muslim world if war came with Germany; and *secondly*, to get the Arabs of Palestine to end their rebellion. To the point, on April 11, 1939, the British Ambassador in Cairo had reported that the Egyptian "Prime Minister said that tranquillity could be restored at once in Palestine if [Jewish] immigration were stopped forthwith for a definite period."

The resulting formula was immediately understood as signaling an early end to Jewish immigration—leaving local Jews a permanent minority, always at the mercy of an intolerant Arab majority. Thus, longtime Zionist leader Chaim Weizmann saw this new British policy as "a death sentence for the Jewish People." On April 18, 1939, Prime Minister Neville Chamberlain received Weizmann's warning:

> The proposed liquidation of the mandate and the establishment of an independent Palestine state, coupled with reduction of the Jewish population to one-third of the total and with restriction of the area of Jewish settlement to a small sector of the country, are

> viewed as destruction of Jewish hopes and surrender of the Jewish community of Palestine to the rule of the Arab junta responsible for the [1936–1939] terrorist campaign. Adoption of these proposals is regarded as tantamount to the establishment of a Jewish ghetto in a small corner of the country. Jews are determined to make the supreme sacrifice rather than to submit to such a regime.

During the May 23, 1939 debate in the House of Commons, Conservative Party back bencher Winston Churchill stood with the opposition parties in vigorously rejecting the Conservative government's White Paper. Churchill emphasized that the UK had made a solemn promise to world Jewry—namely, to the Jewish People globally—that Jews would be able to settle in Palestine. He said the UK as Mandatory Power was entitled to regulate entry but had no right to permanently terminate Jewish immigration:

> What sort of National Home is offered to the Jews of the world when we are asked to declare that in five years' time the door of that home is to be shut and barred in their faces? [...] After that the Arab majority, twice as numerous as the Jews, will have control, and all further Jewish immigration will be subject to their acquiescence, which is only another way of saying that it will be on sufferance. What is that but the destruction of the Balfour Declaration? What is that but a breach of faith? What is it but a one-sided denunciation ... of an engagement?

By contrast, Chamberlain thought looming war with Germany urgently argued for favoring Arabs both locally and generally to win the support of Muslims everywhere, including in British India. Chamberlain had already confided this motive to Cabinet on April 20, 1939:

We are now compelled to consider the Palestine problem mainly from the point of view of its effects on the international situation. It is of immense importance, as Lord Chatfield [Minister for Defence Coordination] has pointed out, to have the Moslem world with us. If we must offend one side, let us offend the Jews rather than the Arabs.

This was clear calculation of perceived national interest, but also a choice facilitated by prejudice, as Chamberlain revealed in a July 1939 letter to one of his sisters: "No doubt the Jews aren't a lovable people; I don't care about them myself."

1939: a Jewish Right to Migrate to Palestine!

Then still a relatively obscure United States Senator from Missouri, Harry Truman caused to be inserted (May 25, 1939) in the *Congressional Record* a new *Washington Post* article by Barnet Nover tarring the White Paper as additional Chamberlain appeasement after the fashion of the September 1938 Munich Agreement with Hitler and Mussolini. In the *Congressional Record*, Senator Truman himself characterized the White Paper as still one more item to be added "to the long list of surrenders to the Axis powers." A portent of things to come was Truman's own view that the British government "has made a scrap of paper out of Lord Balfour's promise to the Jews."

Also aware of the worldwide Jewish refugee crisis, the Permanent Mandates Commission had every humanitarian incentive to refuse to accommodate UK convenience and prejudice. In June 1939, the Commission unanimously concluded:

The policy set out in the White Paper was not in accordance with the interpretation which, in agreement with the mandatory Power and the Council, the Commission had always placed upon the Palestine mandate.

Moreover, the Commission majority stubbornly refused to concede that consistent with the Mandate's explicit terms and its authors' intentions could be the White Paper proposals likely to lead to early termination of Jewish rights of entry and settlement.

A concurring legal assessment came from famed USA jurist Louis Brandeis who repeatedly discussed Jewish migration to Western Palestine with President Franklin Roosevelt from March to May 1939. Less than six months after retiring from the Supreme Court, Brandeis shared (July 31, 1939) with some fellow Zionists his shrewd prediction that Jews would continue going to Western Palestine despite the White Paper. Asked if such Jewish migration would be "illegal," Brandeis replied:

> The Jewish People consider it legal in view of the fact that any attempt to curtail immigration is in violation of the terms of the Mandate; it may be considered illegal by Great Britain but we Jews consider it to be legal.

Rights of Entry and Settlement Post Second World War

After the Second World War (1939–1945), there were several hundred thousand Holocaust survivors and other Jewish refugees, many tragically trapped in postwar European camps for displaced persons. As early as the July 1945 Potsdam Conference, USA President Harry Truman told UK Prime Minister Clement Attlee: "The American people, as a whole, firmly believe that immigration into Palestine should not be closed and that a reasonable number of Europe's persecuted Jews should, in accordance with their wishes, be permitted to resettle there."

The right of Jews to migrate to Western Palestine quickly became an explosive moral, legal and political issue that troubled the conscience of the Western world. From May 1947 also engaged was the sympathy of the Soviet Union which regularly opposed British policy in the Mideast.

The bitter controversy over Jewish entry prompted creation of the 1946 *Anglo-American Committee of Inquiry Regarding the Problems of European Jewry and Palestine*. Releasing its report on April 30, 1946, President Truman specifically supported recommendations for immediate admission of 100,000 Jewish refugees and for abandonment of the 1939 UK White Paper's core principle that further Jewish entry would depend upon approval by the Arabs of Western Palestine: "I am also pleased that the Committee recommends in effect the abrogation of the White Paper of 1939 including existing restrictions on immigration and land acquisition to permit the further development of the Jewish National Home."

Despite this clear message from Truman, Attlee stubbornly refused to implement the Committee's humanitarian recommendations. On October 10, 1946, Truman forthrightly reminded Attlee that it had been more than a year since Truman had first called for immediate admission of 100,000 Jewish refugees. To this humanitarian plea, the President added legal argument:

> In our view the development of the Jewish National Home has no meaning in the absence of Jewish immigration and settlement on the land as contemplated in the Mandate. We

therefore feel that the implementation of the Mandate, as well as the humanitarian considerations mentioned above, call for immediate and *substantial immigration* into Palestine.

The representative of the UK's contrary view sent a letter to USA Secretary of State George C. Marshall from British Foreign Secretary Bevin (June 27, 1947). This letter registered:

> grave concern at the persistent and successful attempts of Jewish organisations to send Jewish illegal immigrants to Palestine from various European countries . . . My colleagues and I feel very strongly that the organisers of this traffic are ... endangering the peace and security of the Middle East.

Such a powerful indictment matched ugly (and sometimes patently illegal) British enforcement to prevent Jews from entering Western Palestine. For example, in February 1947, the UK government had MI6 launch *Operation Embarrass*. Apart from misinformation, propaganda and dirty tricks, MI6 illicitly detonated explosions on five foreign ships in Italian ports. Moreover, even British Admiralty lawyers were then warning the UK government that the Royal Navy was egregiously violating international maritime law by peacetime interception of foreign-flag vessels on the high seas. Such reckless British disregard for legality only added to the cogency of moral and legal argument on the main point. Namely, preventing Jews from migrating to their own "national home" was inconsistent with the spirit and letter of the League of Nations Palestine Mandate which continued to apply under the regime of the United Nations Charter.

Understandably, Jews replied with clear affirmation of the Jewish People's rights of entry and settlement via persistent migration that made newspaper headlines and heightened international support. From 1945 to 1948, overland or by sea, more than 80,000 Jews were able to successfully enter Western Palestine *in full defiance of British jurisdiction,* though some other Jews came with UK authorization.

UK Pushed Arabs and Jews to War?

After the First World War, the international decision to create "a national home for the Jewish People" from the Mediterranean Sea to the Jordan River (Western Palestine) had not displaced local Arabs. They had a climbing birth rate and reduced infant mortality. Arab migrants from other parts of the Mideast also reinforced their numbers. According to the 1937 Peel Commission Report, interwar overland migration by Arabs into Western Palestine was significantly undocumented and unregulated. From 1922 until 1948, the Arab population of Western Palestine almost tripled, while the Jewish population there multiplied eight times. At the end of 1946, Jews were about one third of the population of Western Palestine.

The trauma of the Second World War had spiritually and materially exhausted the British. Their global empire spectacularly collapsed, bringing full sovereign independence (1946–1949) to Transjordan (Eastern Palestine), India, Pakistan, Sri Lanka, Burma, Ireland, and Israel (Western Palestine).

For example, across 1947 the UK government was struggling with implementation of its fateful decision to divide the territory of British India. This division was an attempt to accommodate Muslims who were around one fifth of the population of the Indian subcontinent. There, partition displaced around fourteen million people and caused circa two million deaths. Nonetheless, the UK government eagerly championed partition for the circa 20 percent Muslim minority of

British India, but not for Western Palestine's circa 33 percent Jewish minority.

Though understandable in terms of the increasingly pro-Arab orientation of the UK's broader Mideast policy, growing British negativity to the local Jewish minority was on balance impractical because:

- revulsion at the Holocaust caused many millions worldwide to believe that concentration-camp survivors and other Jewish refugees had a moral right to immediately migrate to Western Palestine;
- including several million American Jews, there was strong bipartisan and popular USA support for Jewish migration to Western Palestine;
- after Hitler's spectacular defeat, some key countries were alienated by Arabs *publicly speaking like Nazis* when referring to Jews, e.g., at meetings of the new United Nations Organization;
- the self-proclaimed leader of the Arabs of Palestine, Haj Amin al-Husseini (the Grand Mufti) was then internationally odious as a notorious Nazi collaborator;
- as then feared at the USA State Department and the UK Foreign Office, the Jews of Western Palestine really did have some fraternal and ideological ties with the Soviet Union—a decisive diplomatic advantage unavailable to the Arabs or the British;
- Jews generated most of the tax revenue, industry and trade in Western Palestine; and
- the British Joint Intelligence Staff warned Cabinet (April 1946) that, not counting women fighters, local Jews could field an 80,000 man army "well-equipped and trained" and with an "excellent system of communications and intelligence"—by contrast, discounted was the military potential of local Arabs who had not impressed during their failed rebellion (1936–1939).

In the postwar imperial breakup, the UK nonetheless rushed forward to grant full sovereign independence (June 1946) to the large expanse of Eastern Palestine (Transjordan). Eight months later, the UK disingenuously despaired of ever being able to succeed within the confines of that narrow strip (Western Palestine) that was all that remained of the greater Mandate.

The perceived political conundrum west of the Jordan River logically flowed from the final excision of Eastern Palestine and a cynical British *rereading* of the Palestine Mandate. This had originally been intended as establishing a long-term British jurisdiction for developing the national home for the Jewish People *via continuing migration and settlement by Jews throughout Western Palestine*. However, from May 1939, the die was cast. The UK government finally decided to officially *reinterpret* the Palestine Mandate as a ten-year transition toward sovereign independence for local Arabs. Moreover, the British newly argued that local Arabs had *an immediate right* to forever remain the majority in Western Palestine.

1947 UN Proposed Heavy Jewish Immigration

In February 1947, Foreign Secretary Bevin said the United Nations would be asked to *recommend* a solution in the light of a firm UK decision to quickly end its mandatory role. The Foreign Secretary reiterated the UK's unwillingness to use British troops or administration to enforce any UN proposal unless accepted by both Arabs and Jews. In this regard, an accurate *Palestine Post* precis captured the crux of criticism by Soviet Permanent Representative to the United Nations, Andrei Gromyko (November 26, 1947):

> The United Kingdom has also failed morally, because she knew—in fact, it was abundantly clear—that one could not

count on any possible agreement between the Arabs and the Jews. Britain had never shown any true desire fully to cooperate with the United Nations for a solution of the question.

With the UK and some other countries abstaining, more than two thirds of the UN Members then voting in the General Assembly supported the historic partition recommendation (November 29, 1947). This resolution *inter alia* incorporated an explicit provision reflecting President Truman's persistent call for early Jewish migration on a large scale:

> The mandatory Power shall use its best endeavors to ensure that an area situated in the territory of the Jewish State, including a seaport and hinterland adequate to provide facilities for *a substantial immigration*, shall be evacuated at the earliest possible date and in any event not later than 1 February 1948.

Prominently included in this UN resolution were detailed proposals for retaining Western Palestine's economic, currency and customs-tariff unity. However, there was to be a *political* trisection, no later than October 1, 1948. Specifically suggested was a "Special International Regime for the City of Jerusalem" *(corpus separatum)*, where Jews had for decades been the overwhelming majority of the municipal population. Significantly, the UN recommendation specified that Jews would still be able to take up residence in Jerusalem which was then envisioned as one city undivided. Finally, this stillborn 1947 UN plan proposed partitioning the remainder of Western Palestine between "the Jewish State" and "the Arab State."

Shouts of "War" Sparked Mideast refugees

The first Secretary-General of the Arab League, Abdul Rahman Azzam was interviewed by the Egyptian newspaper *Akhbar al-Yom*. The resulting article (October 11, 1947) anticipated the November 29th UN partition recommendation, in relation to which Azzam explicitly promised war:

> I personally wish that the Jews do not drive us to this war, as this will be a war of extermination and momentous massacre which will be spoken of like the Mongol massacre or the Crusader wars.

Partition "would, to say the least, result in bloodshed." This assertion was the prediction or rather the *threat* which Egyptian Delegate Mohammed Hussein Heykal (November 24, 1947) offered the UN Ad Hoc Committee on Palestine:

> If the United Nations decides to amputate a part of Palestine in order to establish a Jewish state, no force on earth could prevent blood from flowing there. Moreover, once such bloodshed has commenced, no force on earth can confine it to the borders of Palestine itself. All the peoples of the Orient would come to the aid of their brothers in Palestine in a race war. If Arab blood is shed in Palestine, Jewish blood will necessarily be shed elsewhere in the Arab world . . . Would the members be acting in a humanitarian way to place in certain and serious danger a million [Mideast] Jews simply in order to save a hundred thousand in Europe or to satisfy the Zionist dream? The Egyptian delegation is giving the world fair warning.

Reacting to the November 29th adoption of the UN General Assembly resolution recommending partition, Secretary-General Azzam's Cairo speech (December 4, 1947) vowed: "When our nation starts a fight it doesn't look forward to its conclusion. We will start and will not stop until victory is achieved and our enemy has been thrown into the sea."

Jews quickly welcomed the November 29 General Assembly resolution recommending partition; Arabs, though, angrily rejected it both in Western Palestine and across the Mideast. Pogroms soon hit Jewish communities in several Muslim countries. Civil unrest also began immediately in Western Palestine. There, growing violence gradually became reciprocal, with Jews eventually giving back as much as they got from local Muslim Arabs and armed infiltrators from neighboring Arab countries. British exit was commonly expected to trigger full-scale war. Still, the UK government reiterated determination to withdraw its army and administration by August 1, 1948, later abbreviated to midnight May 14th.

In the interim, the British mostly ignored the General Assembly's November 29, 1947 recommendations, including via continuation of persistent international and local efforts to prevent Jews (especially those fit for military service) from reaching Western Palestine. The UK attitude toward Western Palestine was "irresponsible," wrote Dean Rusk at the USA State Department. On January 26, 1948, Rusk opined: "British noncooperation amounts to a rejection of the Assembly resolution." The USA Consul General in Jerusalem later corroborated Rusk's view, and on February 9, he reported:

> The British continue to be adamant in their refusal to assist in any shape or fashion the implementation of the partition recommendation. Their officials, generally speaking, cannot get out of Palestine too soon. The [British] Police have no sympathy

for the Jews, and state freely their opinion that the latter will "collect a packet" from the Arabs once the British relinquish the mandate. Many Police add that in their opinion the Jews have "asked for it."

Most in Western Palestine dreaded the coming of war. Local Jews had nowhere else to go; but from late 1947 some Arabs began sporadically increasing their exodus from Western Palestine to neighboring Arab countries, including Transjordan (Eastern Palestine). Just hours after the British departed, soldiers from several Arab States (May 15, 1948) entered Western Palestine, thus keeping their repeated public promises to wage war.

These actions underline the critical point—locally and generally, Arabs themselves made the fateful decisions to vociferously reject the 1947 UN proposal for peaceful partition, and instead shout "war." These two bold Arab choices was the principal cause for several waves of Mideast refugees, specifically:

- about 600,000 Arabs constituting most, but not all, of the Arab population that had been living in those parts of Western Palestine that from 1948 came under the Israel government; and
- about 850,000 Jews from various Muslim and Arab countries, as well as from those parts of Western Palestine that were conquered by the Arab armies.

Genocide and Aboriginal Peoples

Genocide is sadly a recurring topic in Jewish history but also historically linked to the tragic fate of other Mideast Peoples like the aboriginal Armenians and Greeks of Anatolia. Genocide also infamously featured when European-origin populations conquered the aboriginal

Peoples of the Americas. There, relentless European invasion was a bitter process that began at the end of the 15th century and persisted into the 20th century. For example, Europeans massacred the Sioux at Wounded Knee, South Dakota, on December 29, 1890. This cruel experience from the Americas was among the reasons why the UN *Declaration on the Rights of Indigenous Peoples* stipulates: "Indigenous peoples have the collective right to live in freedom, peace and security as distinct peoples and shall not be subjected to any act of genocide."

"Genocide" commonly brings to mind the industrial-scale horror of the Nazi extermination machine that killed six million Jews in 1940s Europe. However, broader is the authoritative legal definition that is provided by the 1948 *Genocide Convention*:

> any of the following acts committed with intent to destroy, in whole or in part, a national, ethnic, racial or religious group, as such: (a) killing members of the group; (b) causing serious bodily or mental harm to members of the group; (c) deliberately inflicting on the group conditions of life calculated to bring about its physical destruction in whole or in part; (d) imposing measures intended to prevent births within the group; (e) forcibly transferring children of the group to another group.

20th-century Mideast Jews Feared Genocide

Local precedents were bloody pogroms that Muslims had launched against Jews in Jerusalem (1920); Jaffa (1921); and especially Hebron (1929), which then received widespread attention internationally, including condemnation at the Permanent Mandates Commission.

Steeped in Mideast politics was Harry St. John Philby, a convert to Islam who *inter alia* served as advisor to the Saudi government. In that capacity, Philby confided (1937) to Jewish Agency Chairman David Ben-Gurion his expert view: "The hatred of Jews among all Arab peoples [is] tremendous, and one could not rule out a slaughter in which all the Jews of Palestine would be annihilated." In that same year, the Peel Commission recorded just such anxieties among local Jews:

> What they most fear is a crystallization of the National Home as it is, leaving the Jews in a permanent minority in Palestine, exposed to the possibility of Arab domination, or even, in certain not inconceivable circumstances, of suffering the same fate that befell the Greeks in Smyrna or the [Christian] Assyrians in Iraq.

Starting from the early 1940s, there were again—as in preceding centuries—major Muslim attacks against Jews, including in Iraq, Tunisia, Libya and Yemen. Thus, even before the November 1947 General Assembly resolution recommending trisection of Western Palestine, some Muslims both locally and generally viewed steadily increasing conflict as a potential way to annihilate Mideast Jewish communities.

The Mufti Revered Hitler, Backed the Holocaust

With an eye to the Holocaust that had just come to an end (1945) in Europe, some Arabs both locally and generally saw military force as "the final solution" to the Jewish question in Western Palestine. Such belief in dealing with local Jews with violence—even genocide, if possible—was significantly inspired by the Grand Mufti of Jerusalem, Haj Amin al-Husseini. He was the most famous Muslim Arab leader during the Second World War, mostly because he made regular Islamist and Arab nationalist short-wave radio broadcasts from Nazi Germany.

On January 20, 1941, Haj Amin wrote to the Führer Adolf Hitler in French using *le néant* (non-existence) and *la catastrophe* (catastrophe) for the imminent fate of the Jews of Western Palestine. The German leader fully reciprocated this gruesome theme in a November 28, 1941 meeting with the Mufti in Berlin, optimistically predicting that, via the Caucasus, the Wehrmacht would reach Western Palestine within a few months. An "absolutely reassured and happy" Haj Amin got Hitler's confidential promise: "The German goal then would simply be the annihilation *(Vernichtung)* of Jewry living in the Arab region under the protection of the British."

Hitler respected Haj Amin because the Mufti had earlier instigated the 1920 Jerusalem pogrom, the 1929 Hebron massacre, and the 1936–1939 Arab rising against the British and the Jews. Later, Haj Amin went to Iraq, where he helped foment the *Farhud* that in June 1941 ruthlessly decimated the age-old Jewish community of Baghdad.

From late 1941 in Nazi Germany, Haj Amin used personal contacts, speeches and short-wave radio broadcasts to encourage Germans and Muslims to kill Jews. He repeatedly called for Nazi aerial bombardment of Tel Aviv. He also strenuously lobbied the governments of East Central Europe to ensure that they would send their Jews to certain death in Poland rather than permit any (even children) to escape from Europe.

After the crushing defeat of Nazi Germany, Haj Amin fled Europe where Yugoslavia sought to indict him as a war criminal. In mid-1946, Cairo warmly welcomed him, where he became chairman, first of the Arab Higher Executive and then of the Arab Higher Committee which *seriatim* claimed to be the legitimate government of the Arabs of Western Palestine. In March 1948, he told the Jaffa newspaper *Al-Sarih* that the Arabs were not simply trying to prevent partition, but "would continue fighting until the Zionists were annihilated."

Ottoman Crimes Benefited the Turkish Republic

In the Mideast, perhaps even more influential than the Nazi Holocaust, was the infamous precedent of successful ethnic cleansing in the early 20th-century Ottoman Empire that simultaneously represented Sunnite Islamic Caliphate that retained the loyalty of most Arabs throughout the First World War. Like Haj Amin, many Arab leaders had served in the Ottoman army or administration. They understood that for strategic reasons the Turks, with help from some fellow Muslims, had ruthlessly killed or brutally displaced more than three and one-half million Ottoman Christians, during and immediately after the First World War.

For example, in 1948 still fresh in Mideast memory were the ghastly Armenian genocide of 1915 and the savage liquidation of the aboriginal Greek communities of the Anatolian littoral in 1922. Eminent Arabs such as Haj Amin were well aware that such Ottoman barbarities not only went mostly unpunished but ultimately benefited the newborn Turkish Republic, by brutally cancelling the aboriginal and self-determination rights of the Greeks and Armenians in Anatolia. Those early 20th-century Ottoman "crimes against humanity" served cold calculations of *raison d'état*, but were also significantly fueled by Muslim fanaticism. This was precisely the contemporary assessment of Henry Morgenthau, Senior, who was in Constantinople as USA Ambassador, during the First World War.

What If the Jews Had Been Defeated?

Were the Jews of Western Palestine slated to go the same way as the aboriginal Armenians and Greeks of Anatolia? As May 1948 approached, there was "serious doubt as to whether the Jewish people in Palestine could themselves control the situation." This opinion was certainly the influential view of George F. Kennan's Policy Planning Staff in the USA State Department, which (January 19, 1948) reckoned:

> Without substantial external assistance the proposed Jewish State cannot be established or exist . . . It is improbable that the Jewish State could survive over any considerable period of time in the face of the combined assistance which would be forthcoming for the Arabs in Palestine from the Arab States, and in lesser measure from their Moslem neighbors.

Subsequent history proved Kennan wrong about the indigenous Jewish capacity to create and sustain a nation-State in part of the aboriginal homeland of the Jewish People. However, had Kennan been correct, Jews there would probably have been annihilated or culled via pogrom and ethnic cleansing. Is this grim assessment just "rear-view" speculation? No, because on March 24, 1948, USA Secretary of State Marshall received from the Office of Near Eastern and African Affairs a memorandum warning: "American public sentiment would insist on armed American intervention if necessary to prevent the slaughter of the Jews in Palestine; such slaughter would take place following British withdrawal unless either American or Soviet troops intervene."

In the same vein, USA Defense Secretary James Forrestal (April 4, 1948) was told by Dean Rusk that, when the British would leave Western Palestine, a likely outbreak of "widespread, violent civil war" might result in the "slaughter of thousands and perhaps hundreds of thousands of Jewish residents." In the event, things turned out rather differently, mostly because nascent Israel was able to overcome long-promised Arab aggression.

Local Christians: the First "Palestinians"?

The age-old Jewish People kept the same name and subjective/objective identity consistently from antiquity. By contrast, the dawn of the 20th century found the perhaps half million Muslim Arabs of the Holy Land without much attachment to the mostly Christian idea of "Palestine," which was then quite literally a non-existent country that seldom featured in Muslim imagination.

By contrast, for reasons already explained, focus on a *remembered* "Palestine" came more readily to the Holy Land's several Christian minorities. By circa 1900, local Christians were perhaps no greater in number than the Jews. For more than a millennium and a-half, the old Mideast Christian sects there had been infamous for their bitter hatred of Jews. For example, after the 7th-century CE Muslim conquest of Byzantine Palestine, Christian chroniclers shifted blame to Jews for persecutions of Christians perpetrated by Muslims there.

Historically characteristic of Mideast Muslim governance was the ethno-religious communal autonomy of the Ottoman *millet* system. Whatever its advantages in terms of more or less communal self-government; the *millet* system contributed to sustaining stubborn *inter se* rivalries and resentments among the non-Muslim minorities who were subject to the sultan. Such competition and discrimination facilitated Ottoman "divide and rule." For example, consider the testimony of James Finn who was British Consul at Jerusalem from 1845 to 1863. Finn believed that "Oriental Christians have so great a prejudice and superstitious hatred of Jews, that they would not on any account have dealings with them." A half-century later, Finn's eyewitness report was corroborated by Yusuf Pasha's 1899 letter:

In Palestine, there are also fanatical Christians, especially among the Orthodox and the Catholics. Because they think that Palestine ought to belong exclusively to them, they are very jealous of the progress made by the Jews in their ancestral land. Thus, they never miss a chance to incite the hatred of Muslims against the Jews.

The enduring antisemitism of these old Mideast Christian sects was fueled by dogmatic religious prejudice, perhaps enhanced by continuing economic rivalry. Thus, it is entirely understandable that Arabic-speaking Christians founded two well-known, anti-Zionist newspapers *Al-Karmil* (Haifa, 1908) and *Filistin* (Jaffa, 1911). Those publications perhaps planted some seeds for the post-1967 birth of the specifically "Palestinian" People. But in the short term, those newspapers dovetailed with the fervent anti-Zionism found among local Christians by the USA King-Crane Commission in 1919 and by the UK Peel Commission in 1937.

19th-Century Muslim Arabs "Palestinian"?

Local Muslim Arabs were not generally seen as "Palestinian" by their neighbors or by the increasing number of foreigners who visited the Holy Land. For example, 19th-century European and American travelers sometimes spoke about "a land without a People." This remark was an informed assessment that the few hundred thousand inhabitants of the Holy Land then lacked a distinct, local national identity; but rather had ethno-religious self-identifications similar or identical to those of the adjacent populations, also under Ottoman rule.

Around 1900, local Muslim Arabs significantly had quite a full set of compelling self-identifications that commonly included—family and clan ties; hometown and neighborhood patriotism; an attachment to Greater Syria; a feeling for Ottoman citizenship; a sense of belonging to the ecumenical Muslim community; and pride in both the Arabic language and the Islamic civilization of the great Arab People. For example, Yusuf Pasha's 1899 letter had much to say about the great Jewish People, the Ottoman Empire, Turks and Arabs; and also about Muslims, Christians and Jews in Palestine and beyond. But his 1899 letter said nothing about a distinct *Palestinian* People, exactly because at that time no Muslim Arab population generally self-identified as such.

In the late 19th century, most local Muslims saw "Palestine" as a foreign *geographical reference* with neither historical resonance nor practical advantage given their longstanding self-identifications as "Muslim" and "Arab" due to their very high cultural content. The toponym "Palestine" was relatively unattractive to most local Muslims as a focus for their national self-identification. Local Muslims came to generally self-identify as the distinct "Palestinian" People only after the 1967 *Six-Day War*, i.e., a full twenty years after satisfaction of three necessary preconditions:

- 1917–1922, the *political* rebirth of the name "Palestine";
- 1946, the excision of Eastern Palestine (Transjordan) from the British Mandate; and
- May 14, 1948, close to the last minute, the Jews of Palestine opted to call their new country "Israel."

First Step to a "Palestinian" People: Palestine Reborn

A glance at a 19th-century Ottoman-Turkish dictionary or at Yusuf Pasha's 1899 letter suffices to show that Mideast Muslims were then familiar with the geographical expression "Palestine." However, they generally perceived it to be an indication that was historically Christian, and in usage principally European or Western. More to the point, legally, administratively and politically, there was factually then no State, province or sub-provincial unit called or coextensive with "Palestine." Nor had any such jurisdiction existed for many centuries.

Thus, the first precondition for the eventual emergence of a distinct *Palestinian* People was the stunning political resurrection of the appellation "Palestine." This historical toponym was politically reborn no earlier than the November 1917 Balfour Declaration, which was soon implemented by the 1922 Palestine Mandate of the League of Nations, covering both Transjordan (Eastern Palestine) and the "national home for the Jewish People" (Western Palestine).

History teaches that a People can lend its name to a country. For example, the appellation "England" derives from the Angles, one of the Germanic tribes that settled there during the 5th and 6th centuries CE. A new People can also form by taking its name from an existing country.

For example, about a century *after* the 1867 creation of the Canadian Province of Quebec, the French-speaking inhabitants there suddenly found it expedient to generally self-identify as *Québécois*. With significant political implications, the newborn *Québécois* People is a subset of the larger French-Canadian People that still has some important populations in other places like the Canadian Provinces of New Brunswick, Ontario and Manitoba; and also in the New England States of the USA. This *Québécois* comparison confirms why local Muslim Arabs could not generally self-identify as "Palestinian" until sometime *after* the foundation of a new British jurisdiction called "Palestine."

The *Québécois* comparison also teaches that the birth of a new named People can be triggered by the specific socio-political logic of a particular time and place. In the 1960s, the *Québécois* deliberately stopped being French-Canadian, mostly to better position them for a sustained nationalist attempt to secede from Canada. In the same way and around the same time, most local Arabs purposely transformed themselves into "Palestinians," principally to help their fight against Israel. In neither case does the obvious political motivation invalidate the authenticity of the ethnogenesis. A population is free to generally self-identify as it chooses, and for whatever reasons.

Second Step to a "Palestinian" People: East Palestine Cut from British Mandate

In April 1946, the last Assembly of the League of Nations approved a March UK treaty that on entry into force in June extracted all of Eastern Palestine from the Mandate's territory. This newly-extracted land became an independent Arab State called "the Hashemite Kingdom of Transjordan." This 1946 alteration enhanced the "Palestine" appellation's potential attraction, because for the first time "the Palestine Mandate" now *unambiguously* referred to territory that was fully coincident with the "national home for the Jewish People" (Western Palestine). This smaller Palestine Mandate from the Mediterranean Sea to the Jordan River literally existed for less than two years, i.e., between the births respectively in June 1946 of the Kingdom of Transjordan and in May 1948 of the State of Israel.

From 1922 to 1946, the concept of greater Palestine offered little to help local Arabs fight their war against the Jews; while the status of that smaller Palestine from the Mediterranean Sea to the Jordan River (Western Palestine) was still far too ambiguous to invite any population to generally self-identify by calling itself "Palestinian." For example, during the interwar period:

- Transjordan was explicitly included in (or excluded from) the various treaties which the UK made on behalf of "Palestine."

- The British High Commissioner for Palestine was also empowered to advise the Transjordan Administration, in relation to which he "retained such ultimate powers as the continuance of the Mandate with its international obligations implied."
- The UK "Palestine Command" was under a single British General Officer commanding in both Western Palestine and Transjordan.
- British forces in Transjordan were partly funded by the Palestine government with local revenue that came mostly from Jewish taxpayers in Western Palestine.
- A few Jews served in the Transjordan Frontier Force which answered to the British High Commissioner for Palestine and had been created under legislation of Palestine.
- The Palestine pound was also the official currency of Transjordan.
- The Palestine Railways Administration also operated lines in Transjordan.
- At Palestine's ports and harbors, the trade and commerce of Transjordan enjoyed facilities equal to that of Western Palestine.
- Customs barriers were not to be erected at the Jordan River.
- Nothing prevented Arabs from moving freely in either direction, because the Jordan River was fordable most of the year and, even at official crossing points, there was no need for Arabs to show a passport or identity document.

Extending well to the east of the Jordan River, greater Palestine had enough room for both Arabs and Jews. Before June 1946, the overwhelming majority of local Muslim Arabs did not self-identify as "Palestinian," partly because to have done so then would have signaled not so much a keen desire to destroy the "national home for the Jewish People," as the logical possibility of peacefully distributing the whole of greater Palestine according to the principle of the self-determination of Peoples.

The UK Peel Commission proposed precisely this reasonable expedient in 1937. Recommended at the time was the trisection of Western Palestine : A slice of territory from Jerusalem to the sea near Jaffa was imagined as remaining under British administration. The suggested Jewish State would have extended within a coastal strip from Rehovot to the border with Lebanon, but also thickening north of Afula to take up all the territory abutting Lebanon and Syria. The imagined "Arab State" would have consisted of both Transjordan (Eastern Palestine) and the Arab-inhabited parts of the "national home for the Jewish People" (Western Palestine). This proposal was then reluctantly accepted by Jews but rejected explicitly by Arabs both locally and generally.

Third Step to a "Palestinian" People: The Name "Israel"

Until the afternoon of May 14, 1948, nobody in Washington knew the name of "the new Jewish state." The name "State of Israel" had to be added at the last moment as a handwritten correction to the typed text of President Truman's statement recognizing the provisional government of the nascent country.

For centuries, "Palestine had been a largely Christian term which Jews sometimes used in a mostly secular context. However, during the Mandate period (1922–1948), local Jews were also internationally regarded as "Palestinian" and the adjective was frequently used as synonym for "Jewish." For example, *The Palestine Post* was a prominent English-language newspaper that was the voice of the "national home for the Jewish People," and the Palestine Symphony Orchestra had only Jewish musicians.

Thus, the name "Palestine" and many other specific features of the Mandate regime were still too closely associated with Jews and Zionism to have then been an attractive focus for the national self-identification of most local Muslims. This explains why they did not generally self-identify using the *geographic* indication "Palestinian" until approximately twenty years after May 1948, when Jews had abruptly abandoned the "Palestine" trademark.

"Palestinians" Championed Between the Two World Wars?

Arab leaders were themselves slow to recognize the existence of a distinct *Palestinian* People with its own right to self-determination. For example, no such *Palestinian* People features in the agreement which Chaim Weizmann concluded (London, January 3, 1919) with Prince Feisal as principal Arab leader at the Paris Peace Conference. To the contrary, this document pledges cooperation between greater Palestine imagined as Jewish "territory" and a proposed large Arab State that Feisal then hoped would include the Hejaz, Syria and some other parts of the Mideast. Pertinent to millennial Jewish rights of entry and settlement, the Weizmann-Feisal agreement *inter alia* stipulates: "All necessary measures shall be taken to encourage and stimulate immigration of Jews into Palestine on a large scale, and as quickly as possible to settle Jewish immigrants upon the land through closer settlement and intensive cultivation of the soil."

There is significantly no word about any distinct *Palestinian* People in the strongly anti-Zionist statement for the Paris Peace Conference of the General Syrian Congress, meeting in Damascus. In that important resolution (July 2, 1919), the only "country" championed is "our country Syria." The toponym "Palestine" appears twice and is explicitly defined as nothing more than Syria's "Southern Zone" or "the southern part of Syria, known as Palestine." As for the general reference to "the people of the country," they are decisively *not Palestinians* but rather "our Arab people" and "Arabs inhabiting the Syrian area."

The *Oxford Dictionary of National Biography* says "perhaps no other colonial secretary had as much first-hand knowledge of the colonial empire" as William Ormsby-Gore. His Mideast experience reached back to the First World War when he had soldiered in Egypt and then served in the influential Arab Bureau in Cairo. Responsible to the League of Nations for Palestine as Colonial Secretary, he told the Permanent Mandates Commission in 1937:

> To the Jew, Palestine is *Eretz Israel*—the land of Israel—and he calls it that. To the Arabs, Palestine is an Arab country, part of a new renascent Arab world that for four centuries had been dominated by the Turks and is now a young nation again divided into separate administrations, but with one object in view; to revive once again the glories of Arab medieval civilisation.

Referring to the Arabs of Western Palestine, Ormsby-Gore added: "These people had not hitherto regarded themselves as "Palestinians" but as part of Syria as a whole, as part of the Arab world." The very same insight with regard to pan-Arab national identity had already made it natural for the 1937 Peel Commission Report to recommend that, in the event of partition, the Arab-inhabited parts of Western Palestine ought to be joined to Transjordan (Eastern Palestine). Why? Because the Royal Commission had an abundance of information leading to the conclusion that the Arab-inhabited parts of Western Palestine lacked the economic and fiscal capacity to constitute a sovereign State entirely on its own.

Grand Mufti No "Palestinian" Nationalist!

Nor was a sovereign *State of Palestine* for a distinct *Palestinian* People the preference of the Grand Mufti of Jerusalem before the end of the

Second World War. Though Haj Amin had first gained an international reputation by instigating interwar pogroms and rebellions in Western Palestine, he had strongly believed in *Pan-Arab* nationalism since leaving the Ottoman army during the First World War.

Sure of Axis victory in the Second World War, Haj Amin from August 1940 repeatedly sought from both Fascist Italy and Nazi Germany an early declaration promising Arabs independence, sovereignty and unity—what German diplomats later described as a "great Arab empire." Top Mideast expert at the German Foreign Office, Fritz Grobba judged (November 6, 1941) the principal part of the Mufti's program to be a unified Arab State to consist of Iraq, Syria, Western Palestine and Transjordan. Then excluded from the Mufti's immediate plans was Saudi Arabia where the Germans were courting Ibn Saud as an alternate Arab interlocutor. Also excluded were the Arabs of North and West Africa. By late 1941, the Mufti knew that Mussolini's Italy, Pétain's France, and Franco's Spain each had important African interests that Hitler's Germany then had political and strategic incentives to respect.

At the pinnacle of his power as undefeated master of Europe, Hitler got from the Mufti a January 20, 1941 letter offering Nazi Germany enthusiastic and undying Arab support in return for public recognition of the great Arab People's rights to independence, sovereignty and unity. It is noteworthy that the Mufti's letter touched only incidentally on Western Palestine. He portrayed the 1922 League of Nations Mandate as "English perfidy"—precisely, an intentional "obstacle to the unity and independence of the Arab countries." In the context of the Mufti's much greater Mideast ambitions, the function of Western Palestine was mostly as tocsin for awakening Pan-Arab nationalism: "The question of Palestine has united all the Arab countries in common hatred against the British and the Jews. If having a common enemy is the prelude to the formation of national unity, one can say that the Palestinian question has hastened this unity."

In consecutive Berlin meetings on November 28, 1941, the Mufti pressed first the German Foreign Minister Joachim von Ribbentrop and second Hitler himself for immediate issuance of a declaration on *Arab independence and unity*. However, Hitler personally gave the Mufti reasons to justify a few months delay. Confident that the Soviet Union would soon be defeated, Hitler promised release of the desired *"public appeal to the Arab world"* the instant German armored divisions and air squadrons penetrated south of the Caucasus. That would be the moment of liberation for *"the Arab world"* Hitler told the Mufti.

Did Any Country Champion "Palestinians" in 1947?

In 1947, Arabs locally and generally flatly rejected the UN General Assembly resolution that recommended political trisection, while preserving Western Palestine's economic unity as a single area with respect to economic development, customs tariff, currency, electricity, water conservancy, and transit.

Given such total Arab rejection of the General Assembly resolution, the confidential British diplomatic papers then repeatedly suggested giving Egypt part of the Negev and linking the Arabs of Western Palestine with the new Hashemite Kingdom of Transjordan. This same logic also appealed to the USA State Department. Neither London nor Washington then thought that the Arab-inhabited parts of Western Palestine had the economic, fiscal and military capacity to be a sovereign State entirely on its own. Furthermore, nothing in the diplomatic papers of that time suggested that the British or the Americans then imagined Arabs west of the Jordan River to be a separate *Palestinian* People, as distinguished from Arabs east of the Jordan River.

Similarly, the governments of Egypt and Transjordan then had little regard for the right to self-determination of any distinct *Palestinian* People. Firstly, they had strongly opposed the 1947 General Assembly resolution recommending Western Palestine's trisection. Secondly, no independent Palestinian *State* was ever created between 1948 and 1967, when Egypt held the Gaza Strip and Jordan had East Jerusalem and the West Bank (Judea and Samaria).

The Six-Day War: A Mideast Earthquake?

Egyptian President Gamal Abdel Nasser's Pan-Arabism was one of the principal victims of the Mideast war that erupted on June 5, 1967. Israel's quick victory over several Arab States discredited Pan-Arabism and significantly weakened the drive for Pan-Arab identity. For Egypt, this meant additional focus on its own national self-interest that eventually led to the 1979 peace treaty with Israel, a bilateral agreement that was condemned across the Arab Mideast.

For Arabs of Palestine, the eclipse of Pan-Arabism was reinforced by Israel's conquest of Gaza, East Jerusalem, and the West Bank (Judea and Samaria). This direct Israel presence powerfully enhanced a distinct Palestinian nationalism that had been germinating slowly for about five decades.

After June 1967, local Arabs were far more likely to see themselves as politically distinct from the Arabs of Egypt and Jordan. Now spearheading their own irredentist struggle, local Arabs had fresh incentive to generally self-identify as *"Palestinian."* Moreover, their new leader Yasser Arafat became an international celebrity and the Palestine Liberation Organization emerged as a major player in Mideast politics.

The *additional* self-identification as *Palestinian* was all the more attractive, because it effectively expressed the stubborn determination of local Arabs to eventually master *all* the territory that early 20th-century declarations, resolutions and treaties had explicitly recognized as venue for the "national home for the Jewish People" (Western Palestine).

Nor was this recent *Palestinian* ethnogenesis the first historical instance of a brand-new national identity forged in the fire of bitter ethno-religious hatred and stubborn territorial dispute. For example, consider the significance of the 1930s invention of the name and idea of "Pakistan" for the 1947 emergence of that new country, so solidly based in Muslim identity.

Reconciliation of Rights

This analysis neither denies the current existence of a distinct "Palestinian" People nor suggests that this newborn Palestinian People is today without rights, including claims to self-determination, independence and territory. Rather, there are now "claims of right" on all sides. Urgently required is a *peaceful* process that affects something like a legal or juridical reconciliation of the subsequent rights of the newly-emerged Palestinian People with the prior rights of the age-old Jewish People, including Jewish self-determination rights and longstanding Jewish aboriginal and treaty rights.

Such a reconciliation of rights would have to sincerely respect the honor and dignity of both Peoples. For example, the flawed notion that the newly minted Palestinians might be a "fake" or "contrived" People would not contribute to peaceful reconciliation of respective rights. Nor does it help to feverishly concoct biased legal interpretations that are regularly applied to Israel but not to other countries, in the same or similar circumstances.

The experience of twenty-six centuries teaches that prospects for peace cannot be enhanced by trying to shame the aboriginal Jewish

People in its ancestral homeland. Specifically, neither truth nor justice is served by tarring Jewish settlement west of the Jordan River as "a flagrant violation under international law." *Whatever the source*, such condemnations are mostly political smears that significantly fuel the conflict by providing ideological justification for intransigence, hollow multilateralism, and further fighting.

By contrast, a process for something like a legal or juridical reconciliation of respective rights must be peaceful, inter alia, because the Jewish People's aboriginal and human rights explicitly include the inherent "right to life." Both individually and collectively, Jews have a strong moral and legal right to live safely in Eretz Israel, including throughout Western Palestine which was clearly designated as venue for "a national home for the Jewish People" in treaties from 1922 to 1924. This designation significantly means that the nascent Palestinian People now lacks the right to wage a "war of national liberation" against the aboriginal Jewish People, which is legitimately sited between the Mediterranean Sea and the Jordan River (Western Palestine). There, the Jewish People lives "as of right and not on sufferance," as said by Winston Churchill in 1922.

Sketching a Principled Peace

The political and legal doctrine of the self-determination of Peoples does not require every People to have its own independent State. But, government rests on the consent of the governed, meaning that in principle one People lacks a right to rule over another People. Therefore, a peaceful process for something like a legal or juridical reconciliation of rights would likely respect the doctrine of the self-determination of Peoples which is truly one of the key elements of public international law.

For example, a full-and-final peace treaty agreed *today* would probably have to waive most Jewish aboriginal and treaty rights with respect to land *now* mostly inhabited by Palestinians, wishing to live in a new Palestinian State. By the same principle, such a treaty would probably have to include within Israel land *now* mostly inhabited by Jews. If so, there would be no moral or legal requirement to compensate a new Palestinian State for Israel's retention of some territory beyond the 1949 armistice demarcation lines (ADL):

- Firstly, the ADL were part of the now defunct 1949 Egyptian and Jordanian armistice agreements, both of which clearly stipulated that the ADL were without prejudice to a final political settlement.
- Secondly, no Arab government has ever recognized the ADL as the legitimate and permanent borders of the Jewish State.
- Thirdly, the final peace treaties with Egypt (1979) and Jordan (1994) do not specify the ADL as the international border, but instead explicitly locate the frontier, respectively—to the west, at the 1906 boundary with Egyptian Sinai; and to the east, at the Jordan River.
- Fourthly, the Jewish People's aboriginal, treaty and self-determination rights are juridically so fundamental that they probably outweigh anything that might be said on behalf of the current legal status of the ADL.

Aboriginal rights generally highlight holy places revered by the tribe or People. It is, therefore, easy to imagine that an agreed, full-and-final peace treaty could also draw on Jewish aboriginal and treaty rights to include one or more paragraphs specifically ensuring Jews free, secure and effective access to certain key religious sites, sacred to Judaism for more than two millennia. This might perhaps have some impact in Jerusalem and Hebron, and maybe also in some other venues west of the Jordan River.

The Jewish People's aboriginal, treaty and self-determination rights combine to argue for inclusion in an agreed, full-and-final peace treaty of significant safeguards to ensure that a new Palestinian State could never be a stepping stone to the destruction of Israel. Pertinent to safeguards are some international precedents. For example, including Costa Rica, a score of countries are now without armed forces; and by treaty, Switzerland has been compulsory neutral since 1815. This "safeguards" advice speaks not only politically in terms of national security, but also sounds powerfully in morality and natural and international law.

The moral and legal foundations for recommending some prudential preconditions also refer to the right of self-defence which is a key principle of morality and of almost all legal systems, including public international law. The "inherent right" of self-defence is one of several juridical ways to protect the primordial right to life which features in a variety of authoritative legal sources including the American Declaration of Independence (1776), the Universal Declaration of Human Rights (1948), and the Declaration on the Rights of Indigenous Peoples (2007).

The "unalienable" right to life is understandably of paramount concern to Israel—a country that officially memorializes the Holocaust and is still so often target of dire threats from malevolent Mideast neighbors. For example, consider the repeated public promises to annihilate Israel by the Islamic Republic of Iran, which also works through violent local proxies like Hizbullah, and sometimes via Hamas and even Fatah.

Israel's duty and right of self-defence are also particularly relevant because the Hashemite Kingdom of Jordan volunteered to initiate *major armed attacks from the east* both in 1948 and 1967. Moreover, during the 20th and 21st centuries, major terrorist operations were repeatedly launched both from Gaza and the West Bank (Judea and Samaria).

Including safeguards in an agreed, full-and-final peace treaty is also supported by an argument offered by the famous 20th-century legal philosopher John Rawls. *The Law of Peoples* (1993) says a nascent People's right to national self-determination is neither absolute nor sufficient to justify a morally repugnant purpose: "The right to independence, and equally the right to self-determination, hold only within certain limits . . . Thus, no people has the right to self-determination, or a right to secession, at the expense of subjugating another people." If so, even more compelling is the still stronger argument that no People has the right to self-determination *at the expense of annihilating another People.* Thus, Rawls' logic leads us to the conclusion that it would be immoral, illicit and illegal for Palestinians to cynically exploit a new right to independence *as a way* to destroy the State of Israel, and to eliminate the aboriginal Jewish People which has been in the Mideast for at least twenty-six centuries.

Thus—for moral, legal and practical reasons—an agreed, full-and-final peace treaty would probably need to have a number of major stipulations for Jewish security. Such far-reaching safety measures could embrace transitional or enduring territorial, military and diplomatic provisions. For example, the right to control the airspace west of the Jordan River might perhaps remain with Israel. Moreover, the new jurisdiction might be without army and air force; and also without the right to conclude military alliances with third parties. If so, this would be morally and legally justified because the Jewish People remains a vulnerable aboriginal minority in the blood-soaked Mideast. This region is now an increasingly dangerous place where pogrom, terror, war and genocide are always *just around the corner.*

As specifically expressed in the 1964 Covenant of the Palestine Liberation Organization and the 1968 Palestinian National Charter, the crux of the ongoing dispute is stubborn and enduring rejection of both Jewish *peoplehood* and the millennial history of the Jews in the Mideast. How to address this core of the conflict?

Rights to life and self-defence, explicit Jewish treaty rights, and the doctrines of aboriginal rights and the self-determination of Peoples combine to argue for inclusion of a key test of good faith. Namely, a full-and-final settlement could feature a demographic article unequivocally recognizing the legitimacy and permanence of Israel as *the* Jewish State, i.e., as the political expression of the self-determination of the age-old Jewish People in a part of its aboriginal homeland.

Allen Z. Hertz

Allen Z. Hertz was senior advisor in the Privy Council Office serving Canada's Prime Minister and the federal cabinet, including with respect to aboriginal issues. He formerly worked in Canada's Foreign Affairs Department and earlier taught history and law at universities in New York, Montreal, Toronto, and Hong Kong. Hertz studied European history and languages at McGill University (B.A.) and then East European and Ottoman history at Columbia University (M.A., Ph.D.). He also has international law degrees from Cambridge University (LL.B.) and the University of Toronto (LL.M.).

Israeli "Occupation": The BIG LIE

Sally F. Zerker

The time has come to tell the world's "liars," boldly and forthrightly, that Israeli "occupation" is the BIG LIE of our age. We've all seen the propaganda effectiveness of "the big lie" many times before. This one, too, is working its indecorous distortion of the truth.

The truth is that Jews cannot be occupiers of the Biblical lands, which include present-day Israel, Judea, Samaria, and some of the country of Jordan. The term "occupation" is meant to signify larceny, theft of others' property, abuse of the "Other," cheating, immorality, and dreadful deeds. It is a very offensive concept. Jews are not, and cannot be guilty of these crimes, for two reasons. One, Jews are the extant aboriginal people of this land, and two, Jews have international legal rights to this territory. These two concepts, historical and legal, require elucidation.

What defines Jewish indigenousness is how consistently similar modern Jews are to their ancestors of thousands of years ago. They live in a country with the same name, Israel, such as that which existed in 1312 BCE. Today's Israelis speak the same language that Jews spoke in that land more than 3000 years ago. They do not need a Rosetta stone to understand ancient Hebrew scripts because the language and letters are the same as current Hebrew. Israelis chant from the same biblical texts that their ancestors did millennia past. Their Jewish law —Halachah—derives from their Talmud, which was initially oral and later written down about twenty-five hundred years ago. Their Temple, which was destroyed by invaders twice, can be archaeologically located in their original site in Jerusalem. Moreover, Jerusalem, which was founded by the biblical King David, still stands as the centre of Jewish sovereignty, as it did when King David ruled the Jews.

In reality, the Jewish people established a distinct civilization in their ancient homeland approximately 3500 years ago; Jewish life in Israel today stems from that ancient civilization. Also, despite a series of conquests and expulsions over the centuries, (Roman, Muslim, Crusaders), Jews retained and rebuilt communities in Jerusalem, Tiberius, Rafah, Gaza, Ashkelon, Jaffa, Caesarea, Safed and elsewhere. Years before the Zionist migrations began in the 1870s; Jews lived continuously throughout the land of Israel.

Anthropologist Jose Martinez-Cobo, a Special Rapporteur for the U.N. who studied the place and condition of indigenous peoples and nations, defined such communities of people as those that have continuity with the land, with shared culture in general, such as religion, lifestyle etc., with intrinsic language, with common ancestry, and other relevant factors. By that respected definition of indigenousness, it is irrefutable that Jews are the indigenous people of the land of Israel.

In contrast, there were no Muslims in existence until almost 2000 years after Jews had already settled in Israel because Islam was the religion that Mohammed founded. Arabs, ethnic peoples originating from the Arabian Peninsula, had not come to the region through their conquests until after Mohammed's death in AD 632. No independent

Arab or Palestinian state ever existed in this territory, later called *Palaestina* after the Romans so renamed it in the second century. The Romans changed the name to break the Jews' link with their past after crushing the Jewish revolt in AD 135. Thus, when the Arabs did conquer and occupy parts of the land, they did so as occupiers of previously settled territories by Jews.

Since Jews began immigrating to the region in large numbers in 1882 and onward, fewer than 250,000 Arabs lived in the area, the majority of these having arrived in recent decades. According to many observers and authorities, the vast majority of the Arab population in the early decades of the twentieth century were comparative newcomers, either late immigrants or descendants of persons who had immigrated into the territory in the previous seventy years.

BDS (Boycott, Divestment, and Sanctions) supporters who accept the premise that the Palestinians are indigenous to the land and oppressed by white colonialists have it backward. *National Post* (Canada) columnist Barbara Kay said it well. "It is the (non-white) Mizrachi Jews in continuous habitation in Israel from time immemorial oppressed under a series of imperial regimes, up to and including the British Mandate."[1]

This reference to the British Mandate brings us to the second aspect of Jewish rights to the land of Israel, that of validity under international law. Israel's legal position begins to be established following the First World War, after the Allies defeated Germany, the Ottoman Empire, Austria-Hungary, and Bulgaria. Until then, the Ottoman Empire controlled the entire Middle East and beyond. (The Turks are neither Palestinians nor Arabs). With the Empire defeated; nations and borders that we recognize today in the Middle East didn't exist.

The Allies, (Britain, France, Italy, Japan, and the U.S.), collectively assumed the title The Supreme Council, which then adopted political and judicial power. This council convened the Paris Peace Conference of 1919. In turn, it created the League of Nations that established the Mandate System.

In determining how to assign sovereignty to Middle East territories that includes what are now Israel, Jordan, Syria, Lebanon, and Iraq, the League heard from Arab delegates and Zionist Organizations presenting their respective cases. In April, 1920, in San Remo, Italy, the decision was made. The Arabs were granted sovereignty over 96 percent of the territory, while Jews worldwide were granted Palestine, as per the recommendations of the Balfour Declaration of 1917, which then became international law.

The map drawn up by the San Remo Conference on April 25, 1920, resulted in the creation of new exclusively Arab states; Syria, Lebanon, and Iraq. It also established the borders of the geographic region known as Palestine since Roman times, which was designated for the Jewish National Home to be *reconstituted* there, in consideration of the historical connection of the Jewish people to *Eretz Yisroel* (Land of Israel.)

Notice the decisive language here: it is a *reconstitution*, not a new entity, or a novel creation of a Jewish national home in that territory that includes land east and west of the Jordan River. One alteration occurred in 1922 when the British received permission from the Mandate Authority to carve out a nation from the land of Palestine east of the Jordan River, which was named the Hashemite Kingdom of Transjordan (later Jordan).

This San Remo Resolution, later confirmed in the Mandate for Palestine in 1922, was approved by the 52 members of the League of Nations. The acquired rights of the Jewish people to the land west of the Jordan River are preserved in the UN Charter of 1945 (article 80) and the 1969 Vienna Convention on the Law of Treaties (article 70-lb).

All the countries that exist in the Middle East stem from these Mandates. All the borders we know originate from these Mandates. After the Second World War, the Mandate system was renamed Trustee Council of the General Assembly; they divided the territory of Palestine into six pieces, some granted to the Arabs, some to the Jews. The Jewish portion was significantly smaller than those given to the Arabs. However, the Jews accepted this partition, but the Arabs did not. Had they done so, this partition would probably have become international law.

Instead, there was the War of Independence in 1948–49, when five-plus Arab states attacked the newborn state of Israel. The war ended in an armistice agreement that included the "Green Lines": the line surrounding the portion of Judea and Samaria that Jordan captured, the border around Gaza that Egypt won, and land that Syria captured on the Golan Heights. President Obama treated these lines as legal boundaries, as do the European Union, most ideological leftists, certainly Palestinians and their supporters, and others. However, they have no legal status in international law. They are ceasefire lines. Moreover, they have nothing to do with 1967, except that Israel fought a defensive war then: It was attacked by Egypt, Jordan and Syria; it defeated those invaders, and took back the lands that were captured in 1949.

By calling this land Palestinian territory, we retroactively recognize the Arab conquests by Jordan, Egypt, and Syria. International law prohibits the retention of land acquired through war. There's one exception: territory acquired by winning a defensive war (article 52). Undeniably the Six-Day War was such a war for Israel.

Based on both law and history, Israel cannot be an occupier of any land west of the Jordan River to the sea. The importance of asserting Israel's legal rights is that this alleged "occupation" came to symbolize the justification for Palestinian territorial claims and violence. It is one of those big lies accepted as truth through constant repetition, especially by voices deemed authoritative. Israel as occupier is not only a lie because of the reasons argued here, but also because Hamas controls all of Gaza, and the Palestinian Authority has jurisdiction over the majority of the West Bank, estimated to be as much as 95 percent.

"Occupation" signifies the Palestinians' core political position, namely the rejection of Israel, and is used as justification for the Palestinians' refusal to accept the existence of a Jewish state in any part of the land, to which Jews have a legal right. In this regard, it inhibits the prospect of peace. Let us be clear; anyone using the statement "Israeli occupation" as it relates to the land of Israel is uttering an oxymoron.

Sally F. Zerker

Sally F. Zerker is professor emerita of York University, and a CIJR Fellow. She was the director of Canadian Studies at York. Her Ph. D. was in the field of economics, with an emphasis on economic history. Initially, her work centred on the scholarship of Harold Innis and Canadian economic history: She later applied Innis' analysis into other areas of interest, particularly the political economy of the international oil industry. Her interest in the subject of oil derived from an interest in matters relating to Israel and the Middle East. After her retirement, she worked as a member of the Ontario Energy Board. She was also a founding member of Canadian Professors for Peace in the Middle East,

1975–1995, and co-edited with Prof. Harry Crowe, the *CPPME journal*, Middle East Focus. After Crowe's passing, she took over its editorship. The York University archives house these journals under her name.

1   Kay, Barbara. "Barbara Kay: The indigenous Tribes of Israel," *National Post*, June 28, 2016.

What it Means to Be an Oglala Sioux Jewish Woman: A Personal Account

Mara Cohen

In these days of change, (Aren't they all . . . and haven't they always been) I wanted to share some of my own experience of being born in a liminal place and of a liminal status. Always on the cusp of beginnings and endings, of being between Worlds, and Peoples, and what it means to me as a Jewish Woman of the Oyukpehe Tiyospe "White Horse Creek People," Hehaka Sapa Tiawe "Black Elk," from the Oglala "Scatters Their Own" Band of the Titonwan Lakota "Red Earth People"

In Lakota, the language of my mother's birth people, "Iyeska," has taken on a pejorative meaning—literally meaning "Speaks with white mouth." It was first used to identify the children born of unions between those who came from "over the water" and those who are indigenous to this land. These were the children who could speak both parents' language and who had exposure to both cultures. The Tiyospaye, the Lakota extended Family structure, was one where people intermarried with other Peoples, their Ceremonies allowed family members to "Hunka" "Makes Relatives" from outside, and to make them ours. As the whole World is perceived Lakota Way, to be a vast interconnected web of Relatives, therefore one must Respect all. Subsequently, Lakota perspectives were never exclusionary, nor did Lakotas feel particularly threatened by other people's ways. Either the others were tolerated, or they weren't, as relations with other Tribes and Tribal Histories demonstrated. We had no use for cannibals, human sacrifice or the imbalance created by disrespect. By the Lakota way of timekeeping, we moved from Dog Days, when dogs pulled our Travois, as we followed the herds of buffalo across the Grasslands of the North Plains, to Horse Days, when the Sacred Elk Dog came home. We knew little hunger, and the great blossoming of our Culture happened, and then the heartache of the conquest and the loss of freedom that came with Reservation Days, and the ever-abiding hurt of 1893, and the butchery at Wounded Knee.

This was when the "Iyeska" label had begun to pick up its negative connotations. Often the "Iyeska" used their knowledge of both languages and their relationships with the "other" parent's people, who were now in control, to their personal advantage. And often they encountered the worst of the European prejudices and racism, which they took on as their own, and with which they identified. This is the very definition of being "colonized." We see this happening wherever peoples have been subjected to conquest and dispossessed of their heritage and history. These peoples identify with the oppressor, as the kapos did in the European concentration camps for my father's People. From 1876 until 1978, when the United States allowed the Indian Religious Freedom Act to become law, there were the ongoing depredations of boarding/residential schools where children were taken to assimilate them. The "Kill the NDN; Save the Child" policy of the US government damaged generations that have yet to heal. (NDN is shorthand spelling for Indian.) The forcible removal of Children from their Families, and their Peoples to gut the Cultures and the Identity of these generations, along with the Graveyards filled with Children's remains are just a few of the hallmarks of genocide. The challenge then was bare survival. Humans tend to become very tactical living for the next meal, surviving the next big storm—when the goal is to survive this season, this year—and you can lose hope when there is just more of the same, no future and the sense of valuing who and what they are has been erased.

But there are those who survive, who take a long view, and find what is right for them, despite all they have been through, personally and generationally. My mother was one such indigenous survivor. She rarely spoke of what she had lived through. In fact, not until the evening before she passed did she tell me the worst of it—the rapes, the medical experimentation, the grinding poverty, but also how she had triumphed, finishing university and learned what she needed to know to survive in the world of a dominant culture and make it her own. But she came from a very spiritually focused family, and people whose own spirituality was prescribed though practiced secretly. And then, post Second World War, she found a spirituality that resonated with her and a people she felt at home with, more than any of the other immigrants who had come to North America. She found Judaism. She told me once, "Since all these Peoples didn't seem to like Jews, I wanted to find out why? And I found out that it was because they were a Good People, different than any other."

She spent seven years learning the language, ways of life, traditions, and ceremonies of the Jewish people. And then she understood what an old piece of writing on the thinnest of hide in the old parfleche bag was. A ketubah that was taken in a raid on the Thieve's Road (Bozeman Trail), during the Red Cloud's War. It had belonged to her Mother's, Mother's, Mother. A captive girl. Her cousin sent it to her, and the Rabbi overseeing her study had pictures made. And told her she was a returned person, like the "Lost birds" the taken away, who finally came home. Mother continued her studies. While she knew Jews were indigenous to the Levant, they were also the only group of immigrants who spoke of leaving North America through their prayers and as an understanding of who they are, she had to learn what had been lost to her. Knowing the Spirituality, the Lifeways of your people makes you know yourself, and your relationships with others. As a group who came from Tribes themselves, Jews understood their place as a Family, a great World Family, connected to their past and their future, and remembering as a matter of everyday living. She resonated with this idea on a deeply spiritual level, as she told me, "One of the best things is that Jews are like Lakota in that they don't have to have everybody be just like them. They are who they are, and they know it." She also liked the fact that Jews didn't do the proselytizing "thing," given her own experiences with that.

All this being said, and, as with all things, nothing comes from nothing, and we all come from something. I grew up during the US civil rights movement with the hard-headed pragmatism of being Ranching Folks, along with the cultural dichotomy of the annual visits to my father's family in Seattle. My first perspectives of "white" people were not only of the intolerance of Rapid City, South Dakota for NDN People, and the apartheid prejudices that were faced there but the noisy, verbal, all-encompassing Mizrahi/Sephardi Jewish family I was a part of in Seattle. Always too tall, for that side of my family is short, and their understanding of their piece of the United States versus how we lived in, isolated Reservation Ranch Country. For all the misunderstanding and lack of knowledge about the way of life there (They thought Mom and I lived in a Tipi), they were concerned that the tiny Jewish community in Rapid City couldn't provide enough; enough contact, enough education, enough sense of what it meant to be Jewish in a largely gentile world, amongst Gentile relatives. My great grandma told me story after story of my Jewish family's history. She insisted I learn Hebrew, as well as Arabic and Ladino that were spoken in her home. What she and most of my folks there did not realize, is that it was very, very much like my Lakota family home: The multilingual, ancient oral tradition, as well as story after story of our Lakota history with a high value placed on remembering. Given all of this, I came out essentially a tri-cultural human being. This was a generation before most US citizens had an idea about what that might mean: The ability to see reality from many perspectives. Most importantly, with an ease of movement between different cultures, and rarely seeing the world as "One Way Only," always knowing the exception, and the greatest challenge, being true to all my "selves," and never disrespecting where I come from, or what I learned there. This might have been more difficult had I been born Navajo, or Zuni, traditionally polytheist, but the Lakota perceptions of the world, are what they are, and in very many ways are very similar to Jewish perceptions. Learning to honor both ways within the constraints of the other was hard. And not always knowing my "place" and growing up without the boundaries most have in knowing who they are.

This led to some difficulties in heart and mind; my Jewish faith upheld me through those times. The relationship with the One, and with my Peoples, this gave me the anchor of my fluid existence as a career military member. The tradition of coming from a Warrior People on one side, and as Healers on the other, I found my niche as Flight Nurse, in an Operational Flying Unit. I found a home-away-from-home in any nearby Jewish community wherever I found myself, and in the sketchy, but valuable observances with other Jewish military members in the war zones I worked in. The affinity with other Jewish members of other nation's Military . . . and of course there is Israel.

WHAT IT MEANS TO BE AN OGLALA SIOUX JEWISH WOMAN

As an indigenous person from North America, known as Turtle Island from the traditional Ojibwe reference, I was not prepared for the physical and psychic resonance with the land (Israel) there and had to accept that I was indigenous, though not native there as well. And I know precisely what that means. I uphold those basic obligations in all ways except by making aliyah. And yes, I would give my life for that land and my people there, as I would for this land, and my people here.

Today, the European Left, along with their colleagues in North American academia, and media, the post-liberal, globalist ideology, coupled with the hatred of Jews which is part and parcel of the European cultural matrix, (how could it not be after 1700 years of indoctrination) and which is now in concert with the oil-producing nations and their clients—they are all spilling their cultural and religious agendas and false narratives into the ears of indigenous peoples here. They seek a commonality that is not real. And, to them, ideology is more important than people. As it was with the European communists and the European missionaries, and the European whatever that sought to suborn and homogenize identity, and are as intolerant of others' beliefs as any Spanish Conquistador ever was. And they have used the North American indigenous experience and claimed it for their own. There is some reason they do this, perhaps to gain credibility for their untruths. But I look at the propaganda pictures, the false allegations, and the knowingly misleading memes that so many accept as "reality" when it has nothing to do with the reality on the ground either in Israel, or Judea/Samaria or Gaza. Someday, I will go to Hebron, and see where my family came from . . . I shall not try to take the house back from the Arab family that lives there now. Nor, as I have never lived there, do I regret not doing so up till now. But my Jewish Great Grandma would have. To claim that Jews are "colonizers and occupiers" when they have merely gone back to the land from which they came makes me angry. Jews always lived there, and now they are living there again, despite massacres and ethnic cleansing.

And I am glad. And I hope and pray that Israelis' experiences with their Arab neighbors will improve. That they are not what they were for my Mizrahi Family, that they be not "dhimmi" living under those apartheid laws. I pray that someday the Arab peoples will accept Jewish indigenous rights as being a real thing and that not all peoples have to be Muslim, or ruled by Muslims, and certainly not by Arab Muslims. The Amazigh and Kurds are quite competent to govern themselves, and Arab colonialist culture is just that. In the lands they control, there are no safe minorities if even allowed to remain there at all, and no respect for indigenous peoples or their spiritual traditions.

I have shared my "liminal" experience with you. I hope you do not mind. I see coming, the further destruction of more of the different lenses on the reality that humanity encompasses, in favor of a homogeneous wad—and further loss of generationally-acquired wisdom of different peoples. The new "Liberals" who embrace the idea that all cultures are the equals of all other cultures are insane. Different perspectives, competing ideas, and taking pride in whom and what you are, is not a negative thing. I believe it is the push to eradicate all the "differences" between humans that has proven most dangerous to humanity. And if there is any worse form of governance for Humans than theocracy to be found, I am unaware of it. The Militants of a Hamas or ISIL would see my Traditional Relatives butchered as Pagans ... and the lack of respect for others' lives and ways of life will cause even more loss of the richness of Humanity with the same methods which were used to wipe out Indigenous Religions and Peoples in the Middle East and the Levant. None of what ISIL and Hamas do are new things ... just more firepower and better propaganda excusing what they do ... otherwise, it could still be 637 C.E. with people being buried alive and having their heads hacked off. And they intend to take their show on the road. That is something authentic for all Traditional Indigenous to consider.

Mara Cohen

Mara Cohen was born in 1957 in Seattle, Washington. She is of mixed heritage: Middle Eastern Levantine Jewish from the Island of Rhodes and Sioux, specifically from the Oglala Lakota People. Cohen worked as a Medevac flight nurse, and chief of operational training for a Tactical Operational Group for the United States Air Force and as a cultural linguist specialist served on the Minority Veteran's Advisory Committee for the US Congress and advocates for Indigenous People's Rights.

Simple Truths: A Cree Indian Explains a 2,000 Year Old Rabbinic Teaching

Nathan Elberg

Our Sages teach us that our livelihood is in the hands of God. While we have to go through the motions, our success has little to do with our machinations. Rather, it's a reflection of what God has ascertained is best for us, whether it be immense wealth, terrible poverty, or somewhere in between. All is in the hands of God, and if we want financial success, we should address our request to heaven, rather than to the stockbroker.

It's a simple concept, and an easy principle for a pious person to accept intellectually. But it's much harder to believe in your gut. For example, when you have the opportunity to make extra money by cheating, is that money part of God's plans for you? Conversely, how will God protect your retirement savings when the CEO of the corporation in which you've invested commits massive fraud? If you recite a lot of Tehillim (psalms), is God going to suppress your boss's free will when you ask for a raise?

Two thousand years ago, our Sages taught about our livelihood being in the hands of God. If it rained, the farmers would be successful.

If a Greek or Roman authority overtaxed the people, God could smite him, and solve the problem. If God sent forth the animals, hunters would be successful.

In succeeding centuries, in Babylonia, Spain, eastern Europe and elsewhere, the climate and other natural factors remained strong forces in the economy. Although trade, feudalism and war influenced people's well-being, the connection between livelihood and God was still evident.

With the industrial revolution, the western world turned its devotion to a new deity, progress. This theology placed the illusion of control in the hands of man. For the elite, for those controlling the means of production, the illusion seemed quite real. For the masses of workers, for the peasants, their livelihood became even more capricious. The weight of the burdens of the new taskmasters obscured the hand of God.

Robert Visitor, a Cree Indian living in the small community of Wemindji, taught me the meaning of Chazal's (our sages') teaching about livelihood. I was a young anthropologist, visiting the Quebec coast of James Bay on behalf of the provincial native political association, doing research to fight the James Bay hydroelectric project. Bobby and I had become friends, getting drunk together on the Anglican church's sacramental wine. Over the next few years, as I traveled back and forth to the James Bay coast, I always felt at home at Bobby's, and I tried to make him feel welcome when he visited the urban commune where I lived.

We were spending the winter in the sub-arctic forest in a region that was to be flooded by the hydro project, intending to trap all the fur-bearing animals. The region was physically and technologically isolated. The only roads were the rivers and lakes we paddled, or after freeze-up, walked along.

We had flown into the forest in the early fall. There were seventeen of us: three families, living in a teepee, going out on day-trips to set or check traps and fish nets. Our food was mainly fresh fish, rabbit, partridge, and beaver, supplemented by oatmeal, coffee, tea and flour. Mostly, we lived off the land.

The hunting, fishing, and trapping was successful. Current anthropological research has indicated that many hunting societies lived relatively comfortable lives, much better off than the more "advanced" pastoral or farming societies that succeeded them. As I set rabbit traps, butchered a beaver, and filtered bugs out of the lake water, I had no thoughts about danger, hunger, or God doing anything not nice to me.

One November morning, nobody went hunting. We had freezing rain, and it was impossible to hunt, check fishnets, traps, or anything like that. At best, we could edge down the slippery path to the lake, re-open the hole in the ice, and draw drinking water.

On the second day of freezing rain, again nobody went hunting. No one seemed particularly concerned.

On the third day of freezing rain, I asked Bobby "what happens if the freezing rain keeps up?"

"We starve," he shrugged.

It was an intriguing idea. But, I thought, "what if the federal government lowers interest rates to increase consumer spending? How about if the CEO announces a generous dividend? Lower taxes? Socialist revolution?"

These would not change anything. Nothing man could do would make any difference. If God kept the freezing rain going, we'd starve. If God improved the weather, we'd be fine.

In other words, our livelihood remains in God's hand. Bobby and his fellow Cree understood that teaching at a gut level. It wasn't an idea to be learned and integrated. It's part of the world. We don't have to be taught that the sky is above us, rain falls downward or that we get older over time. The Cree hunters of the northern forest know in the same way that our livelihood is in the hands of God.

Complex economies, high and low technology, and the mythology generated by progress alienate us from this knowledge. We can't know it instinctively, so we must rely on our Torah learning to allow us to grasp the wisdom hidden by the world around us.

Similarly, we shouldn't worry about what we will eat tomorrow. When Bobby said "we'll starve," I could not be as blasé as him. I was concerned and wanted to do something. Bobby knew that our fate was in God's hands, and was quite comfortable with it.

By the age of thirty-seven, he was periodically crippled by arthritis and bad medicine. He attributed arthritis to traveling in the rain in the forest for many days. I blamed the bad medicine on government policies that treated natives as an annoying obligation. The hospital in Montreal had him travel twelve hundred miles to give him cases of aspirin, telling him to take twenty-four pills a day. Maybe the plan was to dissolve his stomach so they wouldn't have to bother with his arthritis, which on some days was so bad that he couldn't move out of bed. I brought him to my doctor, who changed Bobby's diet, eased arthritis, and saved his stomach.

Bobby also had a bad back. When he was a child in a church-run residential school, a teacher heard him speaking Cree, rather than English to a friend. As punishment, the teacher smashed him on the back with a heavy stick. Decades later, when beating and molesting young natives was no longer considered polite, the Chief in Wemindji told Bobby that he should file a claim for the damage he suffered from that punishment; he could probably get ten thousand dollars. As Bobby recounted this to me he was puzzled: what would he do with ten thousand dollars? Why would he need so much money? Bobby meant it. His response wasn't a cliché or a bargaining point with him. It was him.

I've been in business negotiations with some of the wealthiest people in Canada. As they bargained over a transaction, they didn't wonder what difference it would make for them to get a better price: What difference would the extra money make in their life? Bobby, who gave away his money as soon as he got it, who didn't have a bank account or even a phone, was not interested in ten thousand dollars.

In *Pirkei Avot, Ethics of the Fathers*, we are told: "Who is wealthy—he who is satisfied with his lot." It's a theme repeated in folk songs, in movies. . . It's usually written into the song or script by people with lots of money, and according to some is a capitalist plot to keep the poor from complaining about their impoverishment.

Bobby didn't calculate that he could use the money to buy some luxuries for his modest home, take a trip, or purchase a savings bond. Bent over by arthritis, without a penny to his name (and, at the time I last saw him, trying unsuccessfully to recover from a massive heart attack) Bobby was satisfied with what he had. It was his nature.

Bobby took me into his life, he disrupted his family, he traveled a thousand miles for me. If we went by bus, train, or chartered helicopter, it was the same to him. When I bought him an expensive shotgun as a gift, he didn't mind that it only worked properly with expensive shells. Bobby didn't have any money anyway, so whether the ammunition cost a lot or a little was irrelevant.

Bobby was a country & western singer. He considered himself Johnny Cash, but without the cash. He wrote what became a theme song for his people's resistance to the James Bay Hydro Project mentioned above. The refrain was straightforward:

> Building dams on our land is not right
> All the things we have will be destroyed
> If you fellow Indians stand up and fight with all your might,
> If you fellow Indians stand up and fight...

His people signed a multimillion dollar deal with the government, allowing the dams to be built, rivers diverted, hunting grounds flooded. It might have been a good deal had the government lived up to its obligations. Bobby was a bit upset when I satirically re-wrote his theme:

> Building dams on our land is all right
> Though the things we have will be destroyed
> If you fellow Indians stand up and sign with all your might,
> If you fellow Indians stand up and sign...

Pirkei Avot also teaches us that we are obliged to honor our teachers, even a person from whom we have learned only a single letter. Robert F. Visitor was a man of simple wants, uneducated, an alcoholic. He taught me deep truths, not through lessons or lectures, but through living, and I honor his memory.

Nathan Elberg

Nathan Elberg has lived, hunted and trapped with Indians and Eskimos. He has studied folklore, warfare, cannibalism, shamanism, Kabbalah, primitive art, Talmud, Bible, and communications among other things. He worked for thirty years as a commercial real estate broker, as well as published short stories and Torah essays, and blogs occasionally at quantumcannibals.com. His literary sci-fi novel *Quantum Cannibals* was published in 2018 by Double Dragon Press. Elberg is a member of Sci-Fi Canada, has an M.A. in anthropology, and is doing a doctorate in religion.

The David Ahenakew Affair and the Problem of Using the Canadian Justice System in the Fight Against Antisemitism

Ira Robinson

David Ahenakew (1933–2010) was a Canadian First Nations leader whose significant legacy of achievement, including a term as Chief of the Federation of Saskatchewan Indian Nations, and another as National Chief of the Assembly of First Nations [AFN], was compromised by the public expression of his antisemitic feelings. The accusations against him led to two trials on charges of promoting hatred of Jews and to the revocation of his membership in the Order of Canada by the Governor General. The Ahenakew affair has much to say to us concerning antisemitism in Canada as well as the limitations of the judicial process in combatting antisemitism.

According to one version of the story related by Ahenakew, he first learned about "the Jews" as a teenager in Saskatchewan.[1] In Ahenakew's other version, the roots of his attitudes toward the Jews stem from his experience in the Canadian Forces from 1951–1967. While stationed in Germany in 1957, according to this account, he was exposed to a relatively standard German antisemitic narrative that he accepted as accurate. According to this narrative, as he related it:

> The Second World War was started by the Jews ...The Jews damn near owned all of Germany prior to the war. That's why Hitler came in. He was going to make damn sure that the Jews didn't take over Germany, or even Europe. That's why he fried six million of those guys, you know. Jews would have owned the goddamned world.

He also served with the United Nations peacekeeper force in the Gaza Strip,[2] where it is not unlikely that he picked up a Palestinian anti-Israeli narrative (also held by many contemporary antisemites) that he also adopted. As he stated:

> And look what they're [Jews] doing now; they're killing people in Arab countries. I was there, I was there.[3]

Further into the interview, which constituted the primary evidence against him at his trial, he reiterated:

> Well, because I saw the Jews kill people in, in the Egypt when I was over there. And the Palestinians, the Egyptians, the Arabs generally, eh. I saw them fucking dominate everything.[4]

Finally, he expressed his feeling that Jews controlled things in North America as well:

> ... who in the hell owns many of the banks in the States, many of the corporations, many, well look it her [sic] in Canada, ASPER ... ASPER, he controls the media ... Well, what the hell does that tell you? You know that's power.[5]

All these remarks, which triggered Ahenakew's first trial, were made in a question and answer session after a lecture he gave at a meeting of the Federation of Saskatchewan Indian Nations on December 13, 2002. They were reported by the *Saskatoon Star Phoenix* and were quickly picked up by the Canadian national media. Because of these remarks, Ahenakew was charged with promoting hatred in June 2003.

In a magazine article published soon afterward, he was quoted as once again accusing the media, which he likely held responsible for his troubles, of being controlled by Jews (another critical element in the standard antisemitic narrative): "When a group of people, a race of people, control the world media, something has to be done about it."[6]

When he went on trial in July 2005, Ahenakew attempted to excuse his remarks, blaming them on his diabetic condition, an adverse reaction to a change in medication, and his having drunk some wine previously. Convicted of promoting hatred against Jews, he was fined $1000.00. In the aftermath of his conviction, on July 8, 2005, Ahenakew attempted to accuse the Canadian legal system of bias against First Nations. As he stated:

> My case was as much about racism against First Nations as it was about alleged racism against Jewish people . . . First Nations have never received a fair trial in Canada's judicial system.[7]

On July 11, 2005, he was stripped of his Order of Canada. Ahenakew was quoted as attributing the revocation of his Order of Canada to "the pressure put on the advisory committee by some of the Jewish community, including a letter-writing campaign and the lobbying by the CJC . . . the decision by the Advisory Council is a clear indication of where the power in this country lies."[8]

One year later, in June, 2006, the Saskatchewan Court of Queen's Bench overturned his conviction and ordered a new trial on the grounds that while "Mr. Ahenakew's comments, on any standard, were shocking, brutal and hurtful," the judge had failed to properly take into account the context of Ahenakew's antisemitic statements that came out in an angry confrontation with a reporter, and therefore may not have constituted "willful" hatred.[9]

A new trial was held in 2008, as a result of which Ahenakew was acquitted of the charges against him. In the court's decision, issued in February 2009, Judge Wilfred Tucker characterized Ahenakew's antisemitic remarks as "revolting, disgusting and untrue," but accepted the defense's contention that the confrontational context of the remarks did not constitute intent "to incite hatred."[10] The Crown did not choose to appeal to the Supreme Court of Canada. This decision was a disappointment to the Canadian Jewish Congress [CJC], which supported an appeal.[11] Spokespeople for B'nai Brith Canada [BBC] likewise showed their disappointment as well as their concern as to what the lack of appeal might mean. As B'nai Brith's Frank Dimant stated: "We urge the government to step in and take the opportunity to review hate legislation in light of ongoing manifestations of hate in this country."[12]

The Ahenakew affair certainly brought into focus the presence of antisemitic attitudes among First Nations in Canada. Even though a number of prominent First Nations leaders, like Matthew Coon Come[13] and Phil Fontaine,[14] condemned his antisemitism, other first Nations voices supported Ahenakew. The Federation of Saskatchewan Indian Nations, that served under Chief Ahenakew, proposed Ahenakew's reinstatement as a Senator in that organization, which Ahenakew declined after negative political pressure was exerted.[15] Manitoba aboriginal leader Terry Nelson, who accused the Canadian government of attempting to commit genocide against First Nations, publicly asserted that David Ahenakew was a victim of a Jewish-controlled media.[16] In its 2005 Audit of Antisemitic Incidents, B'nai Brith Canada counted five (out of 829) antisemitic incidents emanating from the aboriginal community, which it attributed to the Ahenakew Affair.[17]

What did the Ahenakew Affair mean to Jews in Canada? First of all, it meant that Jewish leaders were paying more attention to the Canadian First Nations community and listening to their concerns with greater sensitivity. Before criminal charges were filed against Ahenakew, Frank Dimant of *BBC* spoke of the possibility of dealing with Ahenakew not through the ordinary Canadian justice system, but rather through procedures of "Indian restorative justice," involving sentencing and healing circles.[18]

CJC had established relations with representative First Nation organizations like the AFN at least since the 1980s.[19] This response was entirely consistent with its philosophy that discrimination against one group is discrimination against all and that the CJC had an obligation to intervene in larger societal issues, especially those respecting human rights. Nonetheless, in response to the Ahenakew affair, the Canadian Jewish communal leadership seems to have devoted special attention to the First Nations community. CJC President Ed Morgan and CEO Bernie Farber thus met with AFN Chief Phil Fontaine in Ottawa on May 16, 2005.[20] Dennis White Bird, grand chief of the Assembly of Manitoba Chiefs, joined Jewish leaders for a Passover lunch in Winnipeg.[21] Both Morgan and Farber participated in the annual General Assembly of the AFN which met in Yellowknife on July 7, 2005. As Farber stated, "the Ahenakew case has solidified our relations with First Nations." He was further quoted as saying that CJC was cooperating with First Nations on issues like land claims and residential schools. Furthermore, CJC sponsored several trips to Israel by aboriginal leaders.[22]

Morgan's speech to the AFN's General Assembly, held on the very eve of the Ahenakew verdict, dealt in general with things the Canadian Jewish and First Nations communities held in common and how they could better understand each other.[23] In his prepared remarks, Morgan spoke at length concerning the Ahenakew affair and its implications for Jewish-First Nations relationships:

> I cannot help but be moved by how decisively and articulately the messages came to us from aboriginal peoples across Canada in the wake of his [Ahenakew's] ugly rant. We were inundated with calls, e-mails, faxes all conveying the same message of condemnation on the one hand and of solidarity with us on the other. They knew that the pain he had caused, though aimed at one group, had hit a much broader target including their own community and Canadian society at large. They understood the irony of a representative of one minority community that has experienced discrimination targeting another such community for a hateful diatribe. They knew that, in the words of one chief, "silence was not an option", so they spoke ... The Ahenakew affair began with hate but thanks to the aboriginal peoples of this country it ended with ... support, mutual respect, and enhanced friendship.

Morgan concluded this section of his remarks by pledging:

> ... that the Canadian Jewish Congress will be more active on aboriginal issues and we will seek new and creative ways to work together to achieve our common goals. We have much to teach, and much to learn from each other.[24]

Anita Bromberg, *BBC*'s national director of legal affairs, echoed Morgan's Jewish commitment to First Nations when she stated, "But as we have said, there is a silver lining, namely, that we have worked closely with the Aboriginal community to build a Canada based on tolerance and understanding and will continue to do so."[25] Alan Yusim, another *BBC* official, emphasized the excellent relationships the organization has built up with Aboriginal groups across the country. "These relationships are stronger than ever as we move forward with many joint initiatives," Yusim said.[26]

The Ahenakew affair also demonstrated the reasonably consistent difficulty Canadians experienced in prosecuting those accused of fomenting hatred against Jews in the Canadian court system. These attempts stretch back more than a century. The first major litigation of this nature stemmed from a 1910 address by Joseph Edouard Plamondon in Quebec City. He accused the Jews of being ritual murderers, usurers, and enemies of the Church. He further called for the revocation of equal rights for Jews and for their exclusion from the country.[27] As a result of his speech and its subsequent publication, Jewish businesses and the synagogue in Quebec City were vandalized and individual Jews assaulted.[28] There followed a libel action brought against Plamondon by Benjamin Ortenberg and Louis Lazarowitz. At his original trial in 1913, Plamondon was acquitted on the grounds that though he had admittedly defamed "the Jews" in his speech and writings, no single identifiable individual had been libeled. He was, however, ultimately found guilty of defamatory libel by the Quebec Court of Appeal.[29]

In response to Adrien Arcand's antisemitic libels of the early 1930s, a bill was introduced in the Quebec Legislative Assembly prohibiting "the publication and distribution of outrageous subject matter against any religious sect, creed, class, denomination, race, or nationality."[30] This bill received little support outside the Jewish community and

Quebec Premier Louis-Alexandre Taschereau, while strongly condemning Arcand's antisemitism, announced that the proper redress was through the courts.[31] The Jewish community then looked to the courts. A 1932 case, Abugov v. Menard proved that existing laws did not give Jews adequate recourse. The judge vigorously condemned the defendants, calling Arcand's publications "anti-Christian, anti-social, and anti-national," but lamented the fact that he lacked legal authority to issue more than a moral injunction.[32] Taschereau then prepared a bill dealing with issues of hate speech directed against identifiable groups only to withdraw it when Arcand's newspapers stopped publication, due to bankruptcy, in 1933.[33]

Anti-hate legislation in Canada would wait until the 1960s. In 1965, the Canadian government established the Cohen Commission to study the issue of hate speech in Canada.[34] In its final report, the Commission called for a law to protect the community from the "corrosive effects of propaganda." Pierre Elliot Trudeau, one of the members of this commission, spoke of this law in the following way: "Let this law be one step towards the society we seek to build."[35]

In the 1980s, however, critical legal tests of the anti-hate law demonstrated that it had serious shortcomings as an effective weapon against antisemites. In Alberta, James Keegstra was charged in 1984 under Federal hate crime laws. He was convicted but successfully appealed his conviction, arguing that the law was unconstitutional because it violated his constitutional guaranty of freedom of expression.[36] In a landmark 1996 ruling, the Supreme Court of Canada overturned the Appeals Court decision, stating that, while the Criminal Code of Canada's prohibition of public incitement to hatred did indeed infringe on the Canadian Charter of Rights and Freedoms, that infringement was justified and the Court sustained Keegstra's original conviction after over a decade of litigation.[37]

The Keegstra affair overlapped with the case of Holocaust denier Ernst Zundel. Zundel was charged in 1985 with publishing a Holocaust denial pamphlet entitled "Did Six Million Really Die?." Zundel utilized his frequent court appearances in Toronto to argue that he should be free to express his views in print and on his website.[38] Zundel was also initially convicted and appealed. The Appeals court decreed a new trial due to procedural errors. He was re-tried in 1988 and convicted again. The Court of Appeal upheld this decision, and Zundel appealed to the Supreme Court of Canada.

The issue before the Supreme Court was whether section 181 of the Criminal Code infringed "the guarantee of freedom of expression in s. 2(b) of the Canadian Charter of Rights and Freedoms and, if so, whether s. 181 is justifiable under s. 1 of the Charter." In 1992, the Supreme Court of Canada overturned Zundel's conviction for "spreading false news," under section 181 of the Criminal Code, saying that the charge violated his Charter right to freedom of expression. Although the court concluded that Zundel's work did indeed violate section 181 and "misrepresented the work of historians, misquoted witnesses, fabricated evidence, and cited non-existent authorities," the Court's decision was that section 2(b) of the Charter of Rights protects all expression of a non-violent form including expression of minority beliefs that the majority may find false. The Court's decision further found that the Criminal Code's restriction on all expressions "likely to cause injury or mischief to a public interest" was far too broad.

Compared to Keegstra and Zundel, whose overt antisemitic activities and trials went on for decades, the Ahenakew affair seems relatively simple and straightforward. Though the evidence shows that Ahenakew held antisemitic views, as well as disparaging views of other groups, such as Blacks, that he had expressed privately for years,[39] there was only one major public incident lasting a bit more than two minutes. Why, then, all the fuss?

It seems most likely that the rapt attention Jews in Canada paid to this case is directly related to the case coming after the long drawn out frustrations of the Keegstra and Zundel trials. It reflects the Jewish community's concern that the Ahenakew case was yet another in a series of legal precedents set, in the words of *BBC*'s Steven Slimovitch, to "constitute a dangerous precedent in which the standard of conviction could be set inappropriately high."[40] Indeed, in the years since Ahenakew was found not guilty, it was noted that Provincial Attorneys General was reluctant to approve hate crime prosecutions.[41]

Is hate speech legislation in Canada an endangered species? The Ahenakew case is enough to give one pause. On the legal side of things, Slimovitch, national legal counsel of *BBC*, stated in 2008, "There's a precedent-setting value to this case in terms of how hate crimes in Canada will be prosecuted.[42] At the same time, there are voices in the media, like that of Charles W. Moore, who pointedly used the Ahenakew case as a prime example of his opposition to: "the insupportable notion behind 'hate speech' legislation . . . that hateful . . . ideas can somehow be suppressed or eliminated simply by setting up legal mechanisms to punish those who express them."[43] Chris Selly as well, using the Ahenakew prosecution as one of the significant points in his argument concludes:

> But generally speaking, the prosecution of hate speech in this country carries a distinct whiff of futility. The good thing is, forcefully combatting hate speech with true speech is every bit as effective with hate speech laws in place as without. There's nothing to stop any Canadian from taking that approach . . . [that] may now have become a matter of necessity.[44]

Ira Robinson

Ira Robinson is Professor of Judaic studies in the Department of Religion of Concordia University, Montreal, Quebec. He has taught at Concordia University since 1979 and served as the Chair of the Department of Religion. He also serves as Chair in Canadian Jewish Studies and Director of the Concordia University Institute for Canadian Jewish Studies. Dr. Robinson is the President of the Canadian Society for Jewish Studies, past President of the Association for Canadian Jewish Studies (formerly the Canadian Jewish Historical Society) and past President of the Jewish Public Library of Montreal. Dr. Robinson was awarded the *Louis Rosenberg Canadian Jewish Studies Distinguished Service Award* by the Association of Canadian Jewish Studies in recognition of his lifelong contribution to the study of Canadian Jewry. His latest book is *A History of Antisemitism in Canada* (Wilfrid Laurier University Press).

1 "Ahenakew blames Jews for Korean war," *Globe and Mail*, November 29, 2008. http://www.theglobeandmail.com/news/national/ahenakew-blames-jews-for-korean-war/article664128/ [accessed December 5, 2013].

2 "Ahenakew: 'I don't hate Jews, I hate what they do'," *Jewish Tribune*, December 2, 2008, http://www.jewishtribune.ca/uncategorized/2008/12/02/ahenakew. [accessed December 5, 2013]

3 R. v. Ahenakew, July 8, 2005, CJCCC Archives DA 23, Box 7, file 3, p. 4.

4 Ibid., p. 5.

5 Ibid., p. 6.

6   Canadian Jewish media tycoon, Izzy Asper, was specifically named by Ahenakew. See Alex Roslin, "Speak No Evil," *This Magazine* (July-August, 2003) http://www.thismagazine.ca/issues/2003/07/speaknoevil.php. [accessed December 1, 2013]

7   "Ahenakew found guilty," *The Gazette*, July 9, 2005.

8   Paul Lungen, "Ahenakew plays the victim, lashes out at Jewish groups," CJN, July 14, 2005; "Ahenakew found guilty," *The Gazette*, July 9, 2005.

9   "Once it's gone, it's gone," CBC News (January 14, 2008) http://www.cbc.ca/news2/canada/politicalbytes/2008/01/. [accessed December 1, 2013]

10 "Canada native leader cleared in second hate trial," Reuters Canada, February 23, 2009. http://ca.reuters.com/article/domesticNews/idCATRE51M5NZ20090223. [accessed December 1, 2013]

11 In an official CJC News Release, dated February 3, 2008, Congress stated that "it would have preferred an appeal." CJCCC Archives DB 12/46/14.

12 "Ahenakew acquittal throws Canadian hate crime legislation into disarray," *Jewish Tribune*, February 24, 2009. http://www.jewishtribune.ca/uncategorized/2009/02/24/ahenakew-acquittal-throws-canadian-hate-crime-legislation-into-disarray.

13 Matthew Coon Come, letter to editor, *Canadian Jewish News* [CJN], January 2, 2003; David Lazarus, "Coon Come condemns Ahenakew during Shabbat service at Shul," CJN, January 2, 2003, p. 9.

14 Ed Morgan to Phil Fontaine, May 18, 2005. CJCCC Archives DA 19.2, Box 37, file 3.

15 "Ahenakew declines reinstatement following negative government reaction," *Jewish Tribune*, April 14, 2008. http://www.jewishtribune.ca/uncategorized/2008/04/14/ahenakew-declines-reinstatement-following-negative-government-reaction [accessed December 5, 2013]; "Native group faces criticism for reinstating Ahenakew," *Globe and Mail*, April 1, 2008. http://www.theglobeandmail.com/news/national/native-group-faces-criticism-for-reinstating-ahenakew/article669599/. [accessed December 5, 2013]

16 Nick Martin, "Blame Jewish-owned media if Indians kill cops: chief," *The Gazette* (Montreal), May 12, 2005; "Chief meets with Jews," CJN, May 12, 2005. Cf. Ed Morgan to Chief Robert Daniels, April 29, 2005. CJCCC Archives DA 19.2, Box 37, file 3.

17 League for Human Rights of Bnai Brith Canada, *2005 Audit of Anti-Semitic Incidents* (Downsview, 2006), p. 7.

18 Sarah Schmidt, "Indian and Jewish leaders meet," *The Gazette*, January 9, 2003.

19 Gerald L. Gall, "The Danger of Complacency," CJN, September 8, 2005.

20 Ed Morgan to Phil Fontaine, May 18, 2005. CJCCC Archives DA 19.2, Box 37, file 3.

21 AJYB 106 (2006), p. 296. http://www.ajcarchives.org/AJC_DATA/Files/AJYB607.CV.pdf. [accessed January 3, 2014]

22 Kathleen McHugh to Larry and Judy Tannenbaum, May 12, 2008. CJCCC Archives DA 19.2, Box 37, file 3. Paul Lungen, "Ahenakew conviction thrown out, new trial ordered," CJN, January 24, 2008, p. 22; Myron Love, "Former native leader seeks Iran's support," CJN, October 22, 2012, http://www.cjnews.com/news/former-native-leader-seeks-iran%E2%80%99s-support. [accessed December 1, 2013]

23 Cf. Phil Fontaine and Ed Morgan, "Aboriginals, Jews, stand together," *Globe and Mail*, July 12, 2005. http://www.theglobeandmail.com/globe-debate/aboriginals-jews-stand-together/article737467/. [accessed December 5, 2013]

24 Draft Text #3 for an address by CJC President Ed Morgan to the Annual General Assembly of the Assembly of First Nations Yellowknife NWT, July 7, 2005, CJCCC Archives DA 19.2, Box 37, file 3.

25 "Ahenakew, 76, leaves a legacy of hate," *Jewish Tribune*, November 25, 2010. http://www.jewishtribune.ca/uncategorized/2010/03/17/ahenakew-76-leaves-legacy-of-hate. [accessed December 5, 2013]

26 "Ahenakew retrial underway," *Jewish Tribune,* November 25, 2008, http://www.jewishtribune.ca/uncategorized/2008/11/25/ahenakew-retrial-underway. [accessed December 5, 2013]. CfPhil Fontaine, Reuven Bulka, and Sylvain Abitbol,

"Two Solitudes Break their Isolation Together," *Globe and Mail*, July 31, 2008. http://www.theglobeandmail.com/globe-debate/two-solitudes-break-their-isolation-together/article715223/. [accessed July 31, 2008]

27 Gerald Tulchinsky, *Canada's Jews: a People's Journey* (Toronto, University of Toronto Press, 2008), p. 142.

28 Israel Medres, *Montreal of Yesterday: Jewish Life in Montreal 1900-1920* tr. Vivian Felsen (Montreal: Vehicule Press, 2000), p. 125.

29 Richard Menkis, "Antisemitism in the New Nation: From New France to 1950," in Ruth Klein and Frank Dimant, eds., *From Immigration to Integration, the Canadian Jewish Experience: a Millennium Edition* (Toronto: Bnai Brith Canada, 2001), p. 38.

30 Martin Robin, *Shades of Right: Nativist and Fascist Politics in Canada, 1920-1940* (Toronto, University of Toronto Press, 1992), pp. 133-134.

31 Lita-Rose Betcherman, *The Swastika, and the Maple Leaf: Fascist Movements in Canada in the Thirties* (Toronto: Fitzhenry and Whiteside, 1975), pp. 13-19.

32 William Kernaghan, "Freedom of Religion in the Province of Quebec With Particular Reference to the Jews, Jehovah's Witnesses, and Church-State Relations, 1930-1960," doctoral dissertation, Duke University, 1966, p. 101; Martin Robin, *Shades of Right*, pp. 136-137.

33 Bernard L. Vigod, *Quebec Before Duplessis: the Political Career of Louis-Alexandre Taschereau* (Montreal and Kingston: McGill-Queen's University Press, 1986), p. 160.

34 Harold B. Troper, *The Defining Decade Identity, Politics, and the Canadian Jewish Community in the 1960s* (Toronto: University of Toronto Press, 2010), p. 107.

35 Troper, *The Defining Decade*, p. 289.

36 Steve Mertl and John Ward, *Keegstra: the Trial, the Issues, the Consequences* (Saskatoon: Western Producer Prairie Books, 1985), p. 35.

37 http://www.cbc.ca/news/canada/when-is-it-hate-speech-7-significant-canadian-cases-1.1036731 [accessed December 1, 2013] It is worth noting that, in his decision in R. v. Ahenakew of July 8, 2005, Judge J. Irwin invoked the Keegstra case in paragraph 4. CJCCC Archives DA 23 Box 7/3.

38   http://www.zundelsite.org/. [accessed December 1, 2013]

39   Alex Roslin, "Speak No Evil," *This Magazine* (July-August, 2003) http://www.thismagazine.ca/issues/2003/07/speaknoevil.php. [accessed December 1, 2013]

40   Paul Lungen, "Ahenakew conviction thrown out, new trial ordered," CJN, January 24, 2008, p. 22.

41   Joseph Brean, "Repeal controversial hate speech law, minister urges," *National Post*, November 18, 2011. http://news.nationalpost.com/2011/11/18/repeal-controversial-hate-speech-law-minister-urges/. [accessed December 5, 2013]

42   "Ahenakew retrial underway," *Jewish Tribune*, November 25, 2008. http://www.jewishtribune.ca/uncategorized/2008/11/25/ahenakew-retrial-underway. [accessed December 5, 2013]

43   Charles W. Moore, "The Freedom to Be Wrong," *The Gazette*, July 17, 2005. Joseph Brean, "Repeal controversial hate speech law, minister urges," *National Post*, November 18, 2011. http://news.nationalpost.com/2011/11/18/repeal-controversial-hate-speech-law-minister-urges/ [accessed December 5, 2013]; "Ahenakew retrial underway," *Jewish Tribune*, November 25, 2008. http://www.jewishtribune.ca/uncategorized/2008/11/25/ahenakew-retrial-underway [accessed December 5, 2013]; Charles W. Moore, "The Freedom to Be Wrong," *The Gazette*, July 17, 2005.

44   Chris Selley, "The Futility of hate speech prosecutions," *National Post*, March 22, 2013. http://fullcomment.nationalpost.com/2013/03/22/chris-selley-the-futility-of-hate-speech-prosecutions/. [accessed December 5, 2013]

I Walk Two Worlds

Scott Benlevi

I walk two worlds: That of my Sephardi mother's and that of my Native American father's. To be Native means to have a deep and personal connection to the land as well as to the history of my ancestors while being Jewish means observing as many of the religious commandments as possible and living a Jewish life in a Jewish land. So how can I reconcile being both Native American and Jewish? Aren't there cultural and ideological contradictions? Hardly. Many Native traditions mirror traditional Jewish beliefs.[1] As such, every person of mixed background has to find a way to incorporate all aspects of their heritage to fully understand who they are. We no longer live in our parents' times when our Native or Jewish heritage was something to be hidden from neighbors, associates, and potential employers. In today's world, people like me can be who we are and be proud of our diverse backgrounds.

I am Walking Knife, a name given to me by a distant relative who belonged to the Shawnee nation. Here in Israel, I'm Scott Benlevi (and in the synagogue, Shamir ben Togormah ben Avraham). I know who my ancestors were, where they lived, and what they accomplished in life. My 4th great grandfather was born on Shawnee land in the Ohio Valley about 1755 to a Scottish father and a nameless Shawnee mother. He was adopted by the Shawnee after being abducted at the age of eleven in a raid on a Virginia plantation where he served as an indentured servant. When the white man came into the Ohio Valley to steal their land, my people refused to give it up. They opted for citizenship instead, even though the US government stole 90 percent of what they owned.[2] That citizenship provided a gateway to education, which produced generations of lawyers, physicians, educators, and soldiers. Unfortunately, our Native cultural ways went by the wayside in the process. It wasn't until my generation that we, the great-grandchildren, began re-examining our Shawnee pasts.

Do I live and share the same beliefs as my Native ancestors before their 'acculturation'? Hardly. That's not feasible. I don't hunt or fish. (I don't eat meat so I am able to keep kosher more easily.) Neither do I wear animal skins or speak a very good Shawnee. But I do honor the land on which I walk by treating it as if it is my mother, and respect all the creatures *ha'Nefesh ha'Gadol* [God] has placed on this earth to share the land with me. And six days of the week in the morning when I don my *tefillin* [phylacteries] to pray, I always include a prayer for all creatures great and small at the prayer's conclusion. No human being owns the land upon which we walk, only *ha'Nefesh ha' Gadol* does. However, if we treat the world in which we live as if it were our mother, perhaps that Great Spirit will make our life's path even and thorn-free for us. Some are chosen to be stewards of the land: In the Americas, Native peoples managed to live life in a balanced way before the ravages to the land that was brought about through European colonial greed.

Israel, by man-made convention and also, I suspect, through divine intervention, has been revived under the same intent as those of the

Natives—to live a balanced life in harmony with Jewish heritage. Some uninformed people ignorant about history claim that Natives and "Palestinians" share an aspiration to 'returned land'. Hardly. Native people want to see the U.S. government honor their treaty obligation, which it has failed to do over the centuries. Broken treaties led to massive land seizures, land which Native peoples used to feed their tribes. History tells us that Native peoples, in fact, inhabited the land before the Europeans arrived unlike the vast majority of 'Palestinians' whose ancestors were massively imported under the imperialistic, colonial British mandate, which consistently broke the terms of their mandate. History proves that Israel is the land of the Jewish people: Jews inhabited the land long before there were Arabs, Muslims, or Christians in the area. Therefore, any connection to Natives and "Palestinians" is patently false. Yes, I walk two worlds, with ease and convenience. I am a Native, a Jew and, now, a proud Israeli.

Scott Benlevi

Part Sephardi and part American Native, Scott Benlevi, an activist for Native American rights and for Israel, is the only Shawnee Jew living in Israel. Benlevi's connection to the State of Israel began in 1978 when he first visited there. He made Aliyah in 2010. Semi-retired, he works part-time as a hotel co-manager and as a genealogical researcher. Benlevi is a fiercely passionate "ultra-Zionist" who challenges, through blogs, Palestinians' claims to their indigenous right to the land of Israel and the international perception that Israel is illegally occupying the West Bank. He feels deeply connected to the land itself, as well as to its people. "I'm a part of this land now, a part of its future," he says.

1. For more on this subject, see Howard Eillberg Schwartz's article in this publication.
2. See: http://www.ohiohistorycentral.org/w/Shawnee_Indians?rec=631 or http://www.shawnee-tribe.com/History.html.

Conversation with a Métis about Israel

Ryan Bellerose

I have some interesting conversations sometimes. That comes from being Métis. Métis are known as the "bridge people," which means that we are often seen as the go-betweens for white people and Indians. What it means is that we don't fit in anywhere entirely, unless it's with our people or oddly enough another group of people who have been marginalized and oppressed like the Jews.

Anyway, when talking about the commonalities between Jews and Indians, I often deal with some ingrained prejudices. You see, most natives are Christians indoctrinated with prejudices towards Jews. When you add the fact that most people who are fighting for native rights also have a left-wing bias, you add in people that were only told the false narrative of Palestinian indigenous status, as well as surface commonalities.

I work hard to teach people that they have got to look deeper than the surface, because the surface is populated mostly by false narratives based on flawed understandings of history, and that the people who perpetuate those myths do NOT have our best interests at heart; in fact, their arguments are actually extremely damaging to our struggle.

Here is an excerpt from an actual conversation between myself and an Indian friend. Do not be alarmed, it's natural for someone to have opinions like this based on flawed history. But most of my people are very intelligent and once set straight, they often understand very well why what they once believed was incorrect. This conversation was with someone who asked me why I am "always talking about the Middle East and Jews." They were upset that I had said something about Palestinians not wanting peace.

"But Ryan, the Jews are bad people because the bible says they killed Jesus. The priest told me that they are bad people," said an Indian friend of mine whose family was forced into residential schools.

"Umm seriously? I am going to ask you a question and I need you to answer honestly. This same priest who told you Jews were bad people, isn't that the same priest who told you that speaking your own language is evil and that having dark skin is a mark of sin? Did you believe that? Are you evil for speaking Cree and being brown?"

"No of course not, why would I be evil for speaking Cree or being dark that's just who I am, saying that, well that's just stupid."

"So why the hell would you believe the priest who tells you the Jews were bad people? That same priest forgets to tell you that Jesus was Jewish himself, that he was a rabbi; that same priest tells you that you are bad and evil for being who you are, so why would he be telling the truth about one thing and not the other?"

"I never thought of it like that, but you are right, if he's lying about us being bad, then he's probably lying about those Jews too."

"Exactly. Especially given that the priest's entire religion is based on Jewish principles and the teachings of a Jewish person, doesn't it seem odd for them to dislike Jewish people so much?"

"So why do you think that Jews are so much like us? They have pale skin so they are white people and all white people have treated us rough."

"Because whiteness isn't about skin tone, it's about privilege. What if I told you that in all of history, only one people was treated as badly as us by white people? That these people were marginalized, oppressed and treated like second and third class citizens even though some of them, physically, look exactly like most white people? Now, what if I told you that these people who sometimes look exactly like white people, were never allowed to be safe or comfortable and, in fact, every few decades would be murdered and scattered?"

"Seriously? But they looked like white people!"

"Yes, but they were always made aware that no matter how white they might look. Jews were not, in fact, white people and therefore they were always LESSER and not safe because no matter how high they got, they could lose it in a second. Does that sound familiar to you at all?"

"Yeah, that sounds like Métis people, hahaha."

"Yup. So now do you understand why my Jewish friends understand us better than white people? Because they aren't white either, they understand better than anyone how crappy it is to work hard and be marginalized for the blood you carry. But they were given a chance to fight for a state of their own, and they took it. We can learn a lot from them."

"But I thought they stole the land from the Palestinians?"
"Did Indians steal the land from the white man here in Canada?"

"Don't say such stupid things, everyone knows Indians were here before white people, how could we steal what was already ours?"
"Exactly. And the Jews were in Israel for 3,000 years before the Arabs, so you tell me how the Jews are stealing land that was theirs? The Jews were kicked off their land just like we were, with only a few of them staying on their traditional lands just like us, the people who kicked them off their lands were the Arabs who showed up 700 years after Jesus. That's important to know because Arabs come from a place called the Arabian Peninsula NOT the Levant. They were outsiders, like the white people here. So if we regained our lands would we be stealing the land from the white people who kicked us off our land or would we simply be regaining our lands? Because the Jews are returning to their traditional lands, how does one steal what one already owns?"

"I thought Arabs were from there forever. But if they came from somewhere else and just took over, then they are just colonists like white people."
"Yes exactly and that's why arguing that Israel is the colonists and the Palestinians are indigenous should bother you because by making that argument, you are arguing that white people will eventually become indigenous too."

"Wow I never thought of that, white people can't become indigenous just by conquering us, so that means other colonizers can't either. So what if the Palestinians are just Jews who converted to avoid being killed. Aren't they still indigenous?"

"Ok, let me ask you a question if you have mixed blood on two sides, but deny one side's culture, language, and traditions, but adopt those of the other side, and you self-identify as that side, what are you? Really? Are you a mixed blood person or have you completely self-identified with one side? Because to be indigenous you must demonstrate that you have ties to a community, you have indigenous language and culture and religion. If you deny those things and adopt the culture, religion, and language of the colonizer, are you really indigenous anymore?"

"I don't think so, that's like all those Métis who tell everyone they are white."

"Exactly, they don't want to be Indians, so we don't force them to be. It's their choice, but they don't get to say "I'm not an Indian, I'm white, but I'm indigenous." They either are or aren't Indians. Is that clear?"

"Yeah, I have a lot to think about."

A few weeks later, this friend joined some pro-Israel groups on Facebook and elsewhere and asked several questions. Now he wants to be more involved in some of the work I'm doing involving setting up cultural exchanges for Native and Jewish kids. So you see, sometimes, all you need is the right argument at the right time, and you can change hearts and minds.

It's important to remember that even though some Jewish people are pale skinned, they are not in fact white. They were not the people who gave us spoiled rations, stole our land and gave us shiny beads in return. While I hesitate to allow our enemies to define us in any way, we must remember that to the government, all Indians are Indians no matter our blood quantum, and to the enemies of our Jewish brothers and sisters, all Jews are Jews. This reality is a burden we both share, but we share it, and it suddenly becomes way less heavy to bear.

Ryan Bellerose

Ryan Bellerose is a Métis from Northern Alberta. His father, Mervin Bellerose, co-authored the Métis Settlements Act of 1989, which was passed by the Alberta legislature in 1990. This act cemented Métis land rights. Ryan founded Canadians for Accountability, a native rights advocacy group. He is also an organizer and participant in the Idle No More movement in Calgary, Alberta, and a proclaimed Zionist.

Savage and Jew: A Shared Stereotype

Howard I. Schwartz

The ability to see resemblances between ancient Judaism and savage religions was a result, at least in part, of the overlapping stereotypes of savages and contemporary Jews in the European imagination. Sifting through the writings on Judaism and heathenism during the sixteenth and seventeenth centuries, one finds striking similarities between the European conceptions of the Jew and the savage. As a Christian antitype, both were pictured as less than fully human, falling somewhere in the great chain of being between human and ape. The savage and the Jew presented similar problems to Christians. In what ways could these peoples be rescued from their idolatrous practices and converted to the true faith? Not surprisingly, European writers relied on the same vocabulary and images to describe the religious practices of their Jewish contemporaries and the savages discovered in the New World. Jews trafficked with the Devil; they practiced ritual murder, especially the murder of innocent children. Europeans leveled similar accusations at savages. Missionary and travel literature routinely described savage religious practices as devil worship and frequently reported the practice of cannibalism and child sacrifice ... Judaism and savage religions both lacked any redeeming moral qualities.

For these reasons, Europeans used similar language to describe Jewish and savage religious practices. This shared vocabulary is evident, for example, if one compares the seventeenth-century voyage literature on the savage with a similar sort of travel literature on Jews and Judaism. This "travel" literature on Jews and Judaism emerged in England during the early seventeenth century, when virtually no Jews were living in that country. Jews had been expelled from England in 1290, and only a relatively small number of Jews had entered England before the seventeenth century. English travelers who went abroad to other European countries brought back stories of their exotic visits to Jewish synagogues. Even after the Jews were readmitted to England in the mid-seventeenth century, numerous English writers report their visits to the local but still exotic synagogues. These reports are similar in tone and attitude to European accounts of savage religion. Compare, for example, Lescarbot's description of Brazilian religion in 1609 with some English accounts of Judaism from the same century:

> As for the Brazilians, I find by the account of Jean de Léry, that not only are they like our savages, without any form of religion or knowledge of God, but that they are so blinded and hardened in their cannibalism that they seem to be in no wise capable of the Christian doctrine. Also they are visibly tormented and beaten by the devil. . . When one tells the Brazilians that they must believe in God, they fully agree, but by and by they forget their lesson and return to their own vomit, which is a strange brutishness, not to be willing at the least to redeem themselves from the devil's vexation by religion. (1914 [1611], 100–101)

In 1659, Samuel Pepys visited a synagogue during Simhat Torah, a lighthearted Jewish holiday. He has the following to say about that occasion:

> But, Lord! To see the disorder, laughing sporting and no attention, but confusion in all their service, more like brutes than knowing the true God, would make a man forswear ever seeing them more: and indeed I never did see so much, or could have imagined there had been any religion in the whole world so absurdly performed as this.

In 1662, John Greenhalgh also had occasion to visit a synagogue and remarks that "the Jews with their taleisim [i.e., prayer shawls] over their heads presented to the observer a strange, uncouth, foreign and . . . barbarous sight" (Glassman 1975, 96, 139-40).

The fact that Jews and savages were similarly stereotyped in the European imagination helped nourish the theory that the American Indians were originally of Jewish stock. Diego Duran, for example, concludes that the Indians must be descended from the Jews because of the similarities in their "way of life, ceremonies, rites, and superstitions, omens and hypocrisies." Duran also writes that "that which most forces me to believe that these Indians are of Hebrew lineage is the strange pertinacity they have in not casting away their idolatries and superstitions, living by them as did their ancestors, as David said in the 105th Psalm." In a similar argument for their common ancestry, Garcia notes that both peoples were timid, liars, and prone to ceremony and idolatry.

It is not surprising that European "travelers" described the religion of the Jews and savages in similar terms. After all, both savage religion and Judaism served as objects of contrast for European self-understandings, a technique that Hayden White (1978, 151) has called ostensive self-definition by negation. When "the need for positive self-definition asserts itself but no compelling criterion of self-identification appears, it is always possible to say something like: 'I may not know the precise content of my own felt humanity, but I am most certainly not like that.' "In European thought, Judaism and savage religion were often the "that's" in the landscape -which one pointed:

The secondary literature on European views of both savages and Jews emphasizes how each served as foils for European views of Christianity:

> The Indian whom the sixteenth-century voyagers came to know was, more than anything else, a creature whose way of life showed Englishmen what they might he were they not civilized and Christian, did they not fully partake of the divine idea of order... The Indian became important for the English mind, not for what he was in and of himself, but rather for what he showed civilized men they were not and must not be (Pearce, 1967; 4-5)
>
> The stories containing references to Jews, which in many instances were carried over from earlier centuries, could be used to point out the superiority of Christianity over Judaism and to strengthen the faith of Christians who questioned the teachings of the church. The Jews, shrouded in legend, were an excellent foil, and the clerics used them often in their sermons. Thus, if they did not exist in the flesh, their imaginary spirits were resurrected to enhance the power of the church in the eyes of the faithful (Glassman 1975; 29)

Given the overlapping stereotypes of the Jew and the savage and the similar use to which such stereotypes were put, it is not surprising that numerous writers recognized commonalities between Judaism and savage religions. But there were other factors as well that enabled this inchoate anthropology of Judaism to emerge. One of the most important of these was the Bible itself.

The Principle of Monogenesis

According to the biblical account of creation, all humanity derived from Adam, the original human entity whom God had created. All peoples, including even the savages in the Americas, were direct descendants of Adam and Adamic culture. The majority of Europeans who wrote on savage religions, including those discussed above, upheld this biblical premise of monogenesis. Consequently, European writers expected to find similarities between the religion of the savages and the religion of the ancients. Since savages were descendants of the original stock of humankind, savage religion contains traces of the original culture and religion. Indeed, it was only by finding such similarities that these writers believed they could identify the point in time when the separation and dispersion of various peoples had occurred. Such parallels and similarities, therefore, did not pose theological problems for these writers. On the contrary, they confirmed the veracity of the biblical story that all peoples derived from one original stock of humankind.

Writers did disagree on the precise moment in history when the savages of the New World had lost contact with the original human society. Those who believed the separation had occurred after the Jewish revelation treated savage practices and beliefs as corrupted but nonetheless recognizable derivatives of Mosaic Law. Other writers believed the American savages had lost contact with original humanity before the Jewish revelation and consequently the parallels in practice and belief could not be explained as a result of an earlier historical connection. To explain the similarities, these writers repeated the argument used by the early church fathers to explain the commonalities between Christianity and the pagan religions of antiquity. The similarities were the work of the Devil who was actively worshiped by the savages. In competing with God for the allegiance of humankind, the Devil had aped the practices of the divinely revealed religion. The savages' vile and abominable practices and beliefs were bastardizations of the true religion of Jews and Christians. Lescarbot, for example, offers this explanation for why the savages of New France, like the ancient Hebrews, performed certain religious practices following the birth of a child:

> They can render no reason for this [i.e., forcing the infant to swallow grease or oil], but that it is a custom of long continuance: whereupon I conjecture that the devil, who bath always borrowed ceremonies from the Church, as well in the ancient as in the new law, wished that his people, as I call them that believe not in God, and are out of the communion of saints, should be anointed like to God's people, which unction he hath made to be inward, because the spiritual unction of the Christian is so" (1914 [1614 3:80).

It is now evident why a space in European discourse momentarily opened for an inquiry into the commonalities between ancient Judaism and savage religions. Such parallels did not yet pose a danger to the privileged status of revealed religion. The stock explanations available were sufficient to account for the similarities between ancient Judaism and heathenism without undermining the assumption that the Jewish religion had been revealed. These similarities were either the survivals of revealed religion that had been nearly obliterated by the human tendency to superstition, error, and sin, or the work of the Devil who seduced humanity away from God by inventing perverted versions of divine religion.

These first anthropologists of Judaism had no way of anticipating the use to which reason would put their comparisons. They had no way of knowing that they had helped prepare the ground for an all-out attack on the privileged status of Judaism and Christianity. Yet, in pointing to the commonalities between ancient Judaism and contemporary heathenism, these writers had unknowingly fashioned what would shortly prove to be one of the greatest weapons in the rationalist attack on revealed religion (Frantz 1967; Gay 1968, 15). Such commonalities generated a suspicion about the validity of the distinction between revealed religion and superstition. The deists, atheists, and materialists of the eighteenth century pointed to these parallels to prove that the distinction between Judaism and contemporary paganism was untenable.

It was this attack that subsequently made an anthropological discourse on Judaism impossible. Once it became clear that commonalities between the religion of ancient Jews and contemporary savages posed a problem for the unique and privileged status of Christianity, various strategies were devised to neutralize this powerful weapon of the Enlightenment. New schemes were developed to put such a chasm between ancient Judaism and savage religions that subsequent writers would no longer find it meaningful or relevant to draw attention to those similarities that had so intrigued earlier writers. In this way, the space that had momentarily cleared for a serious comparison of ancient Judaism and savage religions disappeared for another two centuries. It is to this attack and recovery that our attention now turns.

Judaism and Paganism in the Light of Reason

As reason emerged as a respected source of knowledge late in the seventeenth century and continued so throughout the eighteenth, nothing remained unchanged in the landscape of European discourse. Facts that previously posed no problem to revealed religion now undermined it. Arguments marshaled in support of revelation now threatened its claim to divine origin. One such reversal involved the use of the observed similarities between ancient Judaism and contemporary and ancient paganism. Both the biblical story of creation and the overlapping religious stereotypes of Jews and savages had created an expectation that such commonalities would exist. But as reason vied with revelation for recognition as the ultimate source of all knowledge, these similarities became a potent weapon in the rationalist critique of revelation.

In the vocabulary of the Enlightenment, revelation referred to the religion of both the Old and New Testaments. For orthodox Christian thinkers, the revelation of the Old Testament verified the truth of the Christian revelation. The New Testament incessantly quoted from the Old to show how various incidents in the life of Christ were foreshadowed in the writings of the Hebrew prophets. The fact that Christ fulfilled the prophecies of the Old Testament provided the proof of his messiahship. The validity of the Christian revelation, therefore, required an affirmation that the Jewish testament was of divine origin. As the Orthodox Christian of Thomas Morgan's Moral Philosopher (1738, 15) puts it, "What I mean by Christianity, strictly speaking, or reveal'd as distinguish'd from natural Religion, is the revealed Truths or Doctrines of Revelation as contained in the Books of the Old and New Testaments."

It is not surprising that in attacking the idea of revelation and traditional forms of Christianity, rationalists felt obliged to ridicule the religion of the Jews. In launching this attack, deists in England, France, and Germany revived the strategies of ancient pagan philosophers who had attacked Christianity by heaping scorn on Jews and Judaism. Anthony Collins (1976 [1724], 26, 31) is representative of this impulse when he notes that if the proofs for Christianity drawn from the Old Testament.

> ... are valid proofs then is Christianity strongly and invincibly established on its true foundations ... because a proof drawn from an inspir'd book, is perfectly conclusive ... On the other side, if the proofs for Christianity from the Old Testament be not valid; if the arguments founded on those books he not conclusive; and the prophesies cited from thence be not fulfilled; then has Christianity no just foundation!

One powerful strategy in the emerging rationalist critique involved pointing out the commonalities between revelation as embodied in the Old and New Testaments and contemporary heathenism. These commonalities generated a series of embarrassing questions for the idea of revelation. If one believed in a Devil, as some defenders of revelation did, how could one be sure that only the rites and beliefs of paganism were the work of the Devil? Perhaps those of Judaism and Christianity had a similar origin. Why should one believe the miracles and prophecies of the Old and New Testaments but reject those claimed on behalf of contemporary savage religions? On what grounds could one confidently affirm the revelation to Moses yet deny revelations claimed by other peoples? Was there any fundamental difference between heathen sacrifices and the rites of sacrifice that God had commanded the Israelites to perform? Why should human sacrifices of savages be treated as abominations when God had sacrificed a son?

Questions such as these helped subvert the longstanding dichotomy between revelation, on the one hand, and paganism, heathenism, or superstition, on the other? From the perspective of critical deists, these dichotomies were problematic because revelation did not have an exclusive claim to truth and because savages did not have a monopoly on superstition. Savages had sometimes discovered the fundamental truths of reason. Revelation, for its part, contained countless practices and beliefs that were antithetical to reason. For rationalists, these facts confirmed their basic contention that reason makes revelation redundant and unnecessary. Everything that one needs to know can be derived by the exercise of reason alone. Otherwise, principles of reason should not have been known to savages who had never been exposed to revelation.

Revelation Has No Monopoly on Truth, Heathenism Is Not the Only Superstition

Rationalists argued that the essential principles of religion could be known through the exercise of reason alone. By exercising that faculty, one could learn that God exists, that one has a duty to worship God, that virtue and piety are the best methods of worship, and that one should repent of one's sins. Since these principles were accessible to all persons through the use of reason, revelation itself was unnecessary. There was no need for God to publish "externally" what could readily be known from the internal light of reason.

The first prong of the deist attack involved the attempt to show that what revelation defined as its own essence was already known or at least accessible to savages. Without any revelation at all, humans in all times and all places could discover those basic articles of religion if only they relied upon reason. This Religion of Nature was, as Tindal puts it, "as old as creation." The basic articles of the Jewish and Christian revelation simply represented a re-publication of principles already known to Adam.

But the similarities between revelation and superstition were formal as well as substantive. Heathens legitimated their religions with precisely the same kinds of "external" proofs used to validate Judaism and Christianity. Miracles, prophecies, revelations, and ancient traditions from the ancestors were invoked by peoples the world over to defend their respective religions.

These similarities, rationalists argued, forced defenders of revelation to adopt a double standard. Their own external proofs were trustworthy; those of other religions were false.

Revelation thus failed to see that what it named as superstition in other religions was also contained in itself. As Voltaire (1962 [1764], 476) succinctly puts it, "It is, therefore, plain that what is fundamental to one sect's religion passes for superstition with another sect." From the rationalist perspective, the similarity between the claims of revelation and heathenism left defenders of revelation with but two options: if they continued to ridicule pagan claims to truth, they would have to criticize the identical kinds of claims made on behalf of revelation. Alternatively, if they continued to verify revelation in traditional ways, they would have to recognize the validity of those claims made by others. Either option signified revelation's demise. The first option would destroy revelation's foundation; the second would necessitate accepting the truth of religions in fundamental disagreement with it.

To Enlightenment thinkers, in the light of reason, the doctrine of election also seemed absurd. According to this doctrine, God had made the divine will be known to specific groups of people, first the Jews and subsequently the Gentiles. But numerous other peoples in the world had not been aware of these revelations. It followed that only the elect would know what to do in order to achieve future happiness. The idea of election thus presupposed an absurd notion of God.

Some deists considered the observance of the Sabbath to rest on an equally ridiculous conception of God. "What strange notions must the bulk of mankind have of the Supreme Being, when he is said to have rested and been refreshed" (Tindal 1730, 227). The doctrines of transubstantiation and the Trinity are other examples of absurdities rationalists found at the very heart of revelation.

In addition to such problematic doctrines, revealed religion contained numerous practices that were as contrary to reason as any found among the heathens. The ancient Jews, for example, practiced circumcision and animal sacrifice, customs as barbaric as the rites of mutilation and sacrifices found in other religions.

Some of reason's most strident supporters went so far as to claim that human sacrifice, a practice so common among savages, was also condoned in the religion of the ancient Hebrews. The fact that Abraham responded to God's command to sacrifice Isaac (Gen. 22) and that Jephthah sacrificed his daughter in fulfillment of a vow (Judg. 11:29-40) indicates that the notion of human sacrifice was compatible with the religion of the ancient Jews (Morgan 1738, 131-33; Tindal 1730, 83; Voltaire 1962 [1764, 325). The idea of human sacrifice was also central to the Christian doctrine that God had sacrificed his own son.

While certain practices of revelation were considered particularly absurd, the deists considered all rites problematic. Any of the practices that had been instituted by revelation and that were not derived from reason (which included all of them) were simply superstitions.

The various rites and ceremonies contained in revelation were not different in essence from those savage practices reported by travelers.

All rites and ceremonies owed their origin to the avarice of priests who introduced such practices under the guise of revelation and thereby made themselves indispensable. "Tis then no wonder the number of Gods multiply'd, since the more Gods, the more Sacrifices, and the Priests had better fare" (Tindal 1730, 8i; see also Herbert quoted in Gay 1968, 35).

As is now obvious, rationalists sought to replace the old dichotomy between revelation and superstition with an alternative opposition, Natural Religion versus superstition:

> It is very well known, that there is, and always have been, two sorts or species of Religion in the world. The first is the Religion of Nature, which consisting in the eternal, immutable Rules and principles of moral Truth, Righteousness or Reason, has been always the same, and must forever be alike apprehended, by the Understandings of all Mankind, as soon as it comes to be fairly proposed and considered. But beside this, there is another sort or Species of Religion, which has been commonly call'd positive, instituted, or revealed Religion, as distinguish'd from the former. And to avoid circumlocution, I shall call this the political Religion, or the Religion of Hierarchy. (Morgan 1738, 94)

This new way of slicing the pie completely subverted the old. In this new scheme, ancient Judaism, Christianity, and paganism met one another and mutually recognized their common nature and origin. Each had a share in Natural Religion and superstition:

> What reason has a Papist, for instance, to laugh at an Indian, who thinks it contributes to his future happiness to dye with

a cow's tail in his hands, while he lays as great a stress on rubbing a dying Man with oil? Has not the Indian as much right to moralize this action of his, and shew its significancy, as the Papist any of his mystick rites, or Hocus Pocus tricks? which have as little foundation in the nature or reason of things. (Tindal 1730, 112)

According to reason, there were simply no grounds for a radical distinction between Judaism and Christianity, on the one hand, and the religion of the heathens or savages, on the other.

In sum, rationalists capitalized on an opportunity made possible by revelation itself Revelation predisposed travelers and missionaries to see resemblances between ancient Judaism and savage religions. Revelation taught that all peoples were descendants of one original human ancestor. That portrayal of human history led explorers and voyagers to the conclusion that religions in the New World had degenerated from religions of antiquity. Moreover, revelation had already generated a stereotype of ancient Judaism that was equally applicable to new heathen practices. In the sixteenth century, adherents to revelation did not yet anticipate the damaging implications of assimilating the religion of the Jews to that of the savages. But not long afterward others did. The deists and other proponents of reason realized that such correspondences presented a serious problem for many of revelation's claims. In their judgment, the similarities between the revealed religions and ancient and modern varieties of paganism indicated that revelation was but another superstition, a fabrication of priests whose intent was self-aggrandizement.

Howard I. Schwartz

Howard I. Schwartz, Ph.D., (Howard Eilberg-Schwartz) is an author, business executive, consultant, and social critic. His provocative writing is inspired by the unusual journey he has made in his life from seminary to Silicon Valley. Trained originally as a rabbi, he went on to receive a PhD from Brown University, and spent the early part of his career as a professor of religious studies, before moving to the for-profit sector, where he has worked for more than ten years as an executive in the high-tech software industry, for both startups and a public company. His award-winning *The Savage in Judaism* (Indiana University) has been recognized for his trend-setting work in biblical studies.
www.HowardISchwartz.com.

There is no Palestine, There are no Palestinians

Dr. David A. Yeagley

In 1974, Dennis Banks, a leader of the new American Indian Movement (AIM) travelled to Vienna to meet with the World Council of Churches. While there, he also met with the Palestinian Liberation Organization, identified as a terrorist group, but having nothing to do with American Indians. Why would there be any meeting between AIM and the PLO?

The American Indian Movement, with a violent and anti-American image, had already established ties and associations with Angela Davis and the Communist Party, the Socialist Workers Party (Minneapolis), the American Labor Party, Cesar Chavez, the Puerto Rican Solidarity Committee, Fidel Castro, Hollywood entertainers, and a host of other new Communist organizations popping up all over the United States. The PLO was considered another anti-American Communist effort, and AIM was trying to identify with the general Communist racial agitation movement that was sweeping the "oppressed" peoples of the Third World. Most of these groups welcomed AIM, for no people like the American Indians could protest as loud against America. AIM quickly became a favorite of the anti-American movements.[1]

When I entered the field of American Indian politics in 2001 and learned the history of AIM, I was appalled. That the American Indian should be used as the mascot of the political low-life of the world was to me intolerable. I had nothing but positive intuitions about the Indian role in American society. Indians are an integral part of the land, like the rivers and mountains—more than the Europeans will ever be. The American national image can never be complete or sound without the American Indian being a fundamental part of it. This idea must be put forth positively and not in a confrontational way. Some Americans have a profound respect for Indians. The "Communist" (Socialist, Leftist, Liberal, and Progressive) use of aboriginals, though, seems to have obscured these natural psychological affinities. In demonstrating the Indian's natural affection for the land, the Indian can be seen as the bedrock of patriotism to the land.

I denounced the protracted and paid belly-aching on the part of AIM and condemned its influence as detrimental to Indian youth. Such a negative outlook as was being professionally pushed by Communist-funded (now we call "liberal" or "Democrat") anti-American, anti-constitutionalists was impossible and dangerous. To my mind, nothing poisoned youth more that this nasty disposition of "I've been wronged," and "You owe me." It crushed every natural aspiration of youth. It stifled the intuitive ambitions of young people, particularly young men. Then, as early as 2002, I began hearing of attempts to actually equate the "plight" of the so-called "Palestinians" with that of the American Indian. I found this bizarre. I could not perceive the association. Implied by this, of course, was that Israel was somehow the equivalent of the European invaders of the American continent. So it seemed the Indians were cast against the Jews. This was preposterous, in my opinion.

However, what really struck me was the absolute ignorance of who the so-called "Palestinians" really were, which allowed for the berserk claims that there was a natural connection between American Indians and "Palestinians." By this time, of course, most people knew nothing of the origins of the American Indian Movement, and its anti-American roots, nor of the earliest attempts of associating it with "Palestinians." My work was cut out for me. I had to expose, at least to my audience that consists of conservatives and patriots of all ethnicities and nationalities, the world over who the "Palestinians" were, and why they should not be associated with American Indians.

The people who are today referred to as "Palestinians" are Jordanian, Syrian, and more recently, a mix of other Arab nationals, and some military mercenaries from various Middle Eastern countries like Iran and groups like Al-Qaeda. "Palestinian" does not refer to a race, language, a culture, a land, or a nation. It is a political fantasy. There is no Palestine, and there are no Palestinians.

The word "Palestine" comes from an ancient Hebrew word, פלשת (pelesheth), which has a root meaning "rolling," and means migratory. In Biblical literature, it is first used in Exodus 15:14, identifying the land and inhabitants who would greatly fear the approach of the children of Israel as Israel came up from Egypt. It was a general term for a general area and people. However, in other ancient, non-Hebrew records, the land (or people) is not referred to as such, but separate tribal inhabitants are named, or the names of their 'kings,' such as Kummuhu, Urik, Sibitti-be'l, Enil, Panammu, etc. Tiglath-Pileser III (744–727) left such an inscription.[2] Apparently, the eastern coast of the Mediterranean was an evolving identity, being a highly coveted real estate, yet, until inhabited by Israel, never saw an established nation over any significant period of time.

In the Torah, the same land is also called Cana'an. Cana'an was, however, just another tribe inhabiting the area. There were Hittites,

Girgashites, Amorites, Cana'anites, Perizzites, Hivites, and Jebusites (Deuteronomy 7:1). The list varies slightly elsewhere in the Torah (e.g., Exodus 33:2), but Cana'an is a consistent reference. The land of Cana'an was the land of promise. It was promised to Abraham (Genesis 17:8).

"Palestine" has also been occasionally associated with the word Pi-liš-te, or Philistine. The ancient Hebrew word is פלשתי (pelishtee), which is very similar to pelesheth (Palestine). This People, believed to be Egyptian in origin, did inhabit and dominate the coasts, certainly around the eleventh and tenth centuries BCE. Obviously, they were not part of the original migrants at the time of the Exodus.

None of these ancient peoples who inhabited Palestine prior to the Jews were Arab, nor were they part of any other nation. They were very loosely confederate "fertility cults" with no political focus. When the children of Israel came upon the land, these tribes for the first time experienced a circumstantial unity, which comprised fear of a common enemy.

At the time of the destruction of the 2nd Temple (70 CE), there was, contrary to popular Christian belief, no major or significant dispersion of Jewish people. A small number of Christian Jews left the country for Peraea (a Transjordan province). The Jews, in general, did not leave the country. A new Jewish educational system was immediately established by the famous Rabbi Johannan ben Zakkai. As a people, Israel retained its identity. The Roman armies of Titus destroyed only Jerusalem and the national government. The people and the culture remained.[3] (Without a national government, without a Temple, the coming centuries saw a certain lack of national Jewish focus in the land of Cana'an (Palestine). By the time of the Second World War (1945), the migration of European and Russian Jews to Palestine struck the uninformed world as a radical move. Arab peoples had inhabited Palestine for some time, people from Jordan, southern Syria, and even some Egyptians. It was all a leftover Muslim effect from the medieval era (7th century AD). The Arab Muslims made a profound claim not only on Palestine but on the very site of the 2nd Temple. This, of course, is the historically established Muslim procedure—to take over, to claim someone else's land, to coerce the inhabitants, and to deny other national identities. There is no intent to respect, not to honor, but only to destroy that which is not Islamic.

The modern history of Palestine, as a British land management project (which included the etching out artificial borders of Arab countries all over the Middle East), is found in a fabulous volume by Joan Peters, called *From Time Immemorial* (1984). As in no other work, Peters documents all. The Arab Muslim "refugees" in Palestine, "victims" of the Jewish invasion, were mostly Jordanian and Syrian and were not allowed back into their own countries, but rather were used as tools, as pricks, on the side of the new Israel. Indeed, some of these "immemorial" refugees were declared refugees (by the United Nations Relief and Work Agency) if they had lived in Palestine a minimum of two years before the 1948 conflict.

Rosemary Syigh wrote in 1977 that "a strongly defined Palestinian identity did not emerge until 1968, two decades after expulsion." Peters comments, "It had taken twenty years to establish the "myth" prescribed by Musa Alami."[4] Musa Alami (1897–1984) was an Arab leader born in Jerusalem. Peters quotes him as saying in 1948, "The people are in great need of a 'myth' to fill their consciousness and imagination."[5] Alami wrote in 1949, "How can people struggle for their nation when most of them do not know the meaning of the word? ... The people are in great need of a 'myth' to fill their consciousness and imagination."[6]

Palestine is not a country. "Palestinian" does not denote a language, a religion, a culture, or an ethnicity. It is a myth, indeed. It is a political vision and the most ill-founded, perverted money laundry in modern times. That even someone as noble and broad-minded as Benjamin Netanyahu must speak of "Palestinians" as if they are a legitimate people demonstrates how effective anti-Zionism and anti-Semitism still is in the world.

As an American Indian, a Comanche from Oklahoma, it may strike some as wholly inappropriate that I should venture to comment on affairs so apparently remote from my own. There is a reason for my indulgence: In 2002, there were journalistic political attempts to associate Palestinians with American Indians, such as "Swallowing all before them," in *The Economist* (October 31, 2002), and "Palestinians and Native Americans" in *Counterpunch* (January 14, 2003), and even crazy home-made web pages like "Colonization and Resistance in North America and Palestine" (2002). These efforts to cast Israel in the mold of a colonial force against the "Palestinians" were loud, and I was piquantly offended. I wrote articles of response, as I mentioned earlier, beginning with a *FrontPageMagazine* piece on April 9, 2002, called "American Indians Aren't Like Palestinians." I've written numerous articles since and published them on BadEagle.com, my own website.

I was particularly offended in January 2007, when a group of so-called "Palestinians" actually dressed in pathetic, dime-store American Indian costumes to express their protest to the aggressions of the great Israel. (They were protesting road blocks!) The analogy is amiss. American Indians are not of some foreign race moved into a foreign country, not theirs. We invaded no country. We later did fight a mighty invader, indeed. But we were never asked to go back to our native countries and leave America in peace. Moreover, we did not have billions of other American Indians in surrounding countries ready to come to our aid (or even to use us) and to "wipe America off the map." The analogy of "Palestinians" and American Indians is therefore preposterous, stupid, and reflects the superficial emotionalism of liberals. Liberals profess great sympathy for the poor Indians and decry the horrible abuse of white America wreaked upon the Indians. Liberals use Indians as a symbol, a token of anti-Americanism, anti-patriotism, and anti-white racism, really. That Indians should be also used to support other political groups in the world who claim abuse, as if Indians are the universal mascot of the oppressed, is something I simply cannot tolerate. This places American Indians in the most pathetic, weak, and abject position possible, precluding us from any positive self-image, any development, and any real dignity in the world.

I don't appreciate abuse of American Indians—especially when Indian images are being used to support specific political positions which I reject or despise. My whole purpose in public speaking and writing on political issues in America and in the world is to proffer American Indian history as an example of racial and national honor, not chauvinism, and least of all as a tool to support the antithesis of such. I believe in the preservation of race, nationhood, and honor. In the so-called "Palestinians," I see no race, no nationhood, and no honor.

David Yeagley

Dr. David Yeagley (1951–2014) was a twenty-first century renaissance man. Armed with a doctorate in Music and a Master's degree in Divinity, he attacked issues head on, paying little heed to those offended by his onslaughts. An author, political commentator, classical composer and biblical scholar, he was the conservative voice among American Indian intellectuals. An enrolled

Comanche Indian and an avowed patriot, he railed against those he felt to be a threat to American liberty.

Dr. Yeagley also had a special interest in Persian culture: He published articles on this subject and toured Iran. He was a Judeophile, often expressing his admiration for the Jewish people, the modern state of Israel, and the ancient land of the Bible.

A Bible scholar, Dr. Yeagley, posting on YouTube a series of five minute "Torah Shiurim," (commentaries). When I mentioned to him a concern about a series of verses in the book of Samuel, he quickly brought together other verses which resolved the question.

He was intolerant of people who claimed special privilege based on past or contemporary racial oppression. This earned him the enmity of liberal Indians and their supporters, who denied Yeagley's authenticity as well as his facts. His harsh criticism of many black leaders and especially of their enmity towards American values brought charges of racism. Perhaps there was some truth to this. However, Yeagley also expressed profound admiration for black people who upheld American values, such as Allan West, Herman Cain, and Condoleeza Rice. He said of the latter "Sheer elegance is her draw, and class, to say nothing of intelligence, character, and consistency."

He was also intolerant of people who tried to exploit Native American identity and culture. He ridiculed those who claimed the words "Redskin" or "Indian" to be demeaning and carried both labels proudly. He denounced other ethnic groups who tried to latch on to past exploitation of Indians in order to advance the cause of their own victimization.

Dr. Yeagley had cancer in his youth. The radiation treatments resulted in Mesothelioma when he got older. I called him several times to inquire about his wellbeing, and he could barely catch his breath to say a few words. He was grateful when I told him my synagogue was including him in its prayers for the ill.

Alas, those prayers were insufficient, and he passed away on March 11, 2014. His essay on Palestinian attempts to exploit Indian identity reflects the depths of his scholarship, and the intensity of his passion. While he said much to offend, he said more to inform.

We don't endorse everything that Dr. Yeagley has said during his life. Then again we don't endorse everything the other contributors to this publication have said, either. We choose to let their essays included herein, including Dr. Yeagley's, speak for themselves.

Nathan Elberg

---

1 Alan Stang, "Red Indians," *American Opinion*, September 1975.
2 James B. Pritchard, ed., *The Ancient Near East*, 1973, p. 193.
3 Michael Grant, *The Jews in the Roman World*, 1973, p. 206.
4 Rosemary Syigh, "Sources of Palestinian Nationalism: A Study of a Palestinian Camp in Lebanon," *Journal of Palestinian Studies*, vol. 6, no. 3, 1977.
5 Joan Peters, *From Time Immemorial*, 1984, p. 11.
6 Musa Alami, "The Lesson of Palestine," *The Middle East Journal*, October 1949.

The Convergence of the Native American and Jewish Narratives in our Times

Jay Corwin

In considering the convergence of Jewish and Native American experiences, I may be uniquely suited to this task because my mother was Tlingit of the Eagle moiety and the *kaayaash keiditaan* clan, and my father was Jewish. His father was from Brzesko and his mother from Sniatyn in Galitzia. I am acquainted with both cultures but was born and brought up in Lingít áani, Tlingit territory in Alaska, with my maternal family, and that is my home. I have deep feelings for Jews and Israel, as relatives and as part of my ancestry. I am also an academic, specialized in Spanish and Latin American literature, and it is from a literary sense that I view these convergences of culture and experience.

The first commonalities that come to mind are mass deportations, genocide, harassment, and victimization of all types. For some time, Native Americans, for some time, were projected as exotic philosophical victims of their personal timeless reality. According to a student of mine at the University of Cape Town, Native Americans perceive time differently from Europeans. His professor of Anthropology had stated as much, quoting from some particular expert on the subject. I mentioned that the Mayan calendar is more accurate than any other, which contradicted his professor's idiotic visions of a people living in a time zone that doesn't exist. I mentioned that my mother and my grandmother didn't have that strange perception of time, to which he answered that they probably were westernized. It took me a few minutes to understand how he could have been so lacking in scepticism and reason that he could look at someone with visible Native American features but deny him his personal experience. It was because he was misled by the romantic fantasies of a third-rate thinker with the title "professor." It is at this point that contemporary Jewish and Native American experiences converge wherein professors, journalists, and politicians present a condescending pseudo-anthropological vision of both groups without questioning their presumed unspoken right to pontificate about every aspect of both peoples' existence, including where they should and should not live. I believe the real nature of this pathological desire to issue decrees stems from a simple religious narrative, the Christian depiction of Jesus, and the subsequent roles assigned by Europeans to themselves and others in our contemporary political reality.

Liberals see Native Americans as the perpetual victim, the sob story of the Americas, the gentle red-skinned people who met Columbus and the Mayflower Pilgrims, whose hospitality they recompensed with treachery and violence, the long-dead heroes of Thanksgiving. Moreover, there is the grand Hollywood narrative of the Great Plains, replete with Italians in cheap wigs and bad makeup that evolved into the equally dreadful "Dances with Wolves," that self-serving fantasy of "the Good White Man" who has come to save the people. Transfer the characters to another place and time, and we have "Lawrence of Arabia," the British equivalent. Both are recycled Lord Jim fantasies wherein a god-like European finds himself revered by little brown people. Moreover, both are reinventions of the Jesus story, European style, in which the blonde haired, blue eyed Jesus is killed by the people he has tried to save.

Martyrdom is evident in the story of Jesus, and it has crept into fiction, where it is a sin that condemns a novel or short story to second rate status. It also constitutes a kind of generic formula in the media. There are probably many reasons for that. I suspect that the main one is that media moguls and journalists understand that to make money their task is to manipulate the naïve, not to record history as it occurs. It is an infantile polarization of Good and Evil, a reductionist, condescending narrative technique that serves as a basis for mass media reports. One may only be a hero, a victim or a villain in the comic book realm. In popular media, journalists and activists assume the role of Superman, the saviors of victims and the persecuted. The media is well aware of it. It feeds on the public's longing for a dark, simplistic narrative strategy, inducing in the audience the cheap middle-class thrill of Righteous Indignation.

In today's narrative, Native Americans are placed on the margins, perhaps beyond victimhood. Native Americans are not allowed an equal voice, and never equal footing. I recall a conference in Spain on the indigenous mythology in Latin American fiction, my precise field of expertise. A professor and keynote speaker, a European, had in the course of his presentation presented an analysis of an Aboriginal work of literature, most of which hinged on the meaning of a Quechua word. After he finished speaking, a Peruvian professor challenged his interpretation, explaining that the Quechua word had more than one meaning. Another Peruvian concurred, and the two began discussing the point in Quechua, their native language. The keynote lecturer turned red and in an angry, hostile tone rejected their correction, stating that he had worked with "those people" for over ten years, of course taking ownership of the word and the people. He had probably not counted on the presence of native Quechua speakers in the audience, for how could such humble people be educated, let alone equal to other literary scholars such as himself? I was disappointed to find at such a conference that not one of the keynote speakers was indigenous. What I witnessed was likely a direct result of the European narrative, possibly because that speaker had been induced into this version of literary reality as a child through Karl May's eponymous fantasy novels of a romanticized Navaho named Winnetou.

I am confident that the man who offered the correction was aware of my unique background. Just after this exchange and without his having asked, I brought him a bottle of water from a vending machine. That isn't something a European would very likely do. (For aboriginals, doing so is a sign of respect for someone who is older as well as an acknowledgment of his linguistic expertise and his rank as a distinguished professor and authority on his language (Quechua). Simply nodding is not enough whereas bringing someone a drink in this context is a sign of servitude.) This was also a subtle nod to him that I also acknowledged his victory over an under-prepared opponent.

That anecdote is also illustrative of the victim/perpetrator narrative. Because, while the victim is pitied, he may never be equal, and for him to ask for or demand equality means the end of victimhood. The speaker's refusal to acknowledge the correction was not just an indication of his arrogance (after all, how could he be wrong, as he had studied and therefore owned those people) but a reminder to us aboriginals that we are only to be pitied. In a sense, this is a repetition of the story of the crucifixion, the religious subtext to all contemporary European political thought. In other words, it is just not possible for ethnic Europeans to remove themselves from their depiction of

Jesus. Victims are not allowed to play any other role, because then it spoils the entire fantasy. Moreover, he is not entitled to be Jewish: To skirt that minor problem he is relegated like Native Americans to the mythological realm of a non-existent time zone, ascending to Heaven and returning, and presented as one who is closer to God than others and, therefore, no longer human. The image of the crucified Christ, a misunderstood philosophic being who lived in his timelessness, is identical to the insulting mythologized cliché of Chief Joseph, who said: "I will fight no more forever." The false ascription of a lyrical philosopher comes through people too thick to understand that the man was only saying "I will not fight any longer" in a language he hadn't mastered.

Of course, in this narrative and European passion plays Jews incarnate evil. It is the basis of much small-minded European racism. Europe could not have Jews in it, and now, since the establishment of the State of Israel, it cannot allow Jews the sense of equality that all people who live independently in their national homeland must have. It sometimes seems as if the entire planet was given carte blanche by Europeans to express its opinions about Israel. The subtext to those who live in the Diaspora is, "We will only like you and let you into our social circles, you bad Jews, if you condemn Israel." This narrative is reminiscent of the hollow promises of the Spanish Inquisition: You will only be equal if you accept our religion and condemn your people. It is an empty promise, of course, but foolish people still fall for that promise, which is similar to the Euro-American history of broken treaties with Native Americans. After the Spanish Inquisition and over three hundred broken treaties, one would expect us all to wake up and reject the tainted promises of European racists.

The condescending treatment of Jews, forged in Europe, was passed from European Socialists and the All-Embracing emancipated promises of Soviet Socialism to academics and journalists all over the world. In place of Christianity, there is a false, comic-book version of humanism that is broadcast via the mass media that seeks to convert its readers and viewers into the Cult of Righteous Indignation.

An excellent academic might, instead, question why others are trying to press a particular agenda and then consult histories. My impression is that today's journalists have no concept of world history, nor do left-leaning university professors. Instead of reading canonical works they, like Soviet socialists, have created new versions of history, and cite from the babbling brook of postmodern-speak, such as the works of professors who oddly have no formal training in history. While citing these professors, the leftist academics adorn themselves with the socialist rosary in the face of the vampire Zionist: "How can you say we are antisemitic when the people we are quoting are Jews?" Similarly, the Crow were used by Europeans who knew they would gladly help defeat their enemy, the Sioux. These tacticians understand that Jews also have their philosophical divisions and employ the likes of Noam Chomsky and Judith Butler to cite as righteous Jews. Moreover, their new faith of Righteous Indignation allows them a platform to unleash ethnic hatred, as long as it masquerades as criticism of Israel. I noticed that cult members use the word "Zionist" as a curse and an insult.

In North America, anti-Israel demonstrations are all the more absurd. To hear people scream things such as, "Get off their land!" makes me wonder how these people could not be aware of whose land "they" are on. Has post-modern education erased pre-contact American history? A prime example of this sort of blind hypocrisy is the drama of Rachel Corrie, the American anti-Israel activist who fell under an IDF bulldozer on March 16, 2003. Rachel Corrie lived in Olympia, Washington and attended Evergreen College. Her professors encouraged her misconceptions and half-cooked visions of Righteous

Indignation and social justice, revolving around a notion of occupation and stolen land. Some of them publicly claimed that Israel murdered her. In other words, the Jesus narrative is their way of understanding the zoned-out girl whose friends had time to snap photographs of her falling under a heap of the earth as a bulldozer plowed over her, but didn't have time to pull her to safety. Without the crucifixion, there is no passion play, no climax to the narrative, and no means of blaming Jews for the murder of a Holy Martyr. The best analogy I have read compares Corrie with Mary McGregor, the dim-witted school girl in Muriel Sparks' novel *The Prime of Miss Jean Brody*, who is brainwashed by her teacher and dies volunteering in the Spanish Civil War, for the wrong side.

I see Rachel Corrie, her professors and allies as hypocrites of the highest magnitude, as Olympia, Washington was ceded by treaties backed by false promises and lies. In short, the Coastal Salish were defrauded of their land in the 1850s. On that land sits the Corrie family and Evergreen State College where Rachel Corrie was a student. As far as I am aware, no one has yet made this point. While screaming about how Israel mistreats Gazans, Corrie's mere presence on requisitioned (stolen) Coastal Salish land invalidates any claims to martyrdom that her family, political cohort or Arab Nationalists may proclaim.

I often suspect that such people understand that they are guilty of land theft, or at the very least know they are benefiting from bartering in stolen property. To attenuate their guilt, they divert their attention and the attention of others to a mythological version of Gaza. It is much easier to live in a comic book fantasy than to reconcile oneself to the most challenging questions of justice in the present. For me, the Rachel Corrie story represents the convergence of the Native American and Jewish narratives in our times. It is the point at which European myth-making has reached its climax and imploded under

THE CONVERGENCE OF THE NATIVE AMERICAN AND JEWISH NARRATIVES

the weight of its stupidity. It is a story of media generated heroes, villains, and victims, which to any thinking person should recognize as hollow and transparently stale as a Hallmark card.

Much of academia is perverted by left-leaning social activism whose proponents are busy rewriting history or reinterpreting it according to a Soviet-style party line. It calls to mind the anger I felt when reading Tzvetan Todorov's *Conquest of America*, which alludes to European cultural superiority during the fall of Tenochtitlán. In doing so, it conveniently ignores the fact that Tenochtitlán (now Mexico City) was not conquered, as is claimed, but was abandoned by its population who fled a horrific plague, probably smallpox, that ran rampant and killed people in droves, and likely was carried by one of Cortes' co-conspirators. It was an accident of nature and not a victory of superior technology or military tactics that allowed history to unfold as it has, and to claim otherwise is just a lie.

The Leftist Academic narrative which serves as the intellectual force behind BDS is trapped in an infantile phase of development. Leftist academics pretend to reject Christianity while stuck in its mythological mindset, and its need for Jewish villains only reassures us that they are Christians without God, who maintain their form while rejecting the spiritual content and replacing it with a false humanism (though maintaining an overtly Calvinist brand of sanctimonious grandstanding). Replace "Jesus" with "Palestine" and voila, the new religion! I would suggest that the real center of academic leftism is its propensity for dispensing pity to the victims it creates, for without those victims there can be no object of their pity and no feeling of superiority issues as a by-product of acts of Righteous Indignation, like the bad aftertaste of an artificial sweetener.

I contend that Native Americans and Jews were similarly victimized by Europeans unable to extract themselves from the perversion of their desire to be good human beings. This desire was manipulated by the media, by the socialist inheritors of Soviet anti-Israel propaganda and by Arab nationalists, who along with the Soviets, invented a false analogy to Native Americans, based on a desire to dominate Jews rather than coexist. In these terms, our peoples are inextricably bound until we can abate the mythologies that fuel the false Righteous Indignation that impedes us all from progressing in the modern world.

Jay Corwin

Born in Wrangell, Alaska, Jay Corwin has a doctorate in Spanish and Latin American literature from the Florida University and is the author of many pieces of criticism of Latin-American fiction. He is currently head of the Spanish program at the University of Cape Town.

The Indigenous Rights of the Jewish People

Ambassador Alan Baker

The Jewish People

1 There is no doubt whatsoever as to the historical presence and existence of the Jewish people in the Middle-East generally, and the area of historical/Biblical Palestine, or "the Holy Land" in particular.

2 This presence is well-documented and proven not only in the scriptures of all three monotheistic religions, but it is also visible in extensive archeological remains. As well, it is borne out by empirical historical writings and records by early Greek, Roman, pagan and other visitors to the area, dating from the third century BCE and through the third century CE, and by Muslim historians around the eighth century CE, attesting to a continuous Jewish presence.

3 The fact that the sources of Christianity evolved and emanated from Judaism is, in and of itself, further proof of the presence of a thriving Jewish community in the area generally, and in

the specific areas in which the Jews existed from Bible times, including Judea (from which the term Jew stems), Samaria and the other neighboring tribal areas.

4. Of all extant Peoples, the Jewish People has the most substantial claim to be indigenous/aboriginal to the Holy Land, where Judaism, the Hebrew language, and the Jewish People were born around 5,000 years ago. Before then, the Holy Land was home, *inter alia*, to the immediate ancestors of the Jewish People, including the Phoenicians, Ammonites, Moabites, Edomites, and Philistines. Those other peoples have long since vanished from the world.

5. More recent historical documentation regarding the re-establishment of the Jewish Home in the area, including the 1917 Balfour Declaration and statements by Winston Churchill and others during the 1920s, recalls the historical connection of the Jewish People with Palestine.

6. Judaism, the Hebrew language and the Jewish People, was already established in the Holy Land before the 6th-7th century CE emergence of Islam and Classical Arabic and the initial Muslim conquest of the Holy Land in the first half of the 7th century CE.

7. There is no doubt as to the historic nature of the Muslim presence as well as its rights to the area since the 7th century CE, and the more recent continuous residence of Arabs in the areas of Judea and Samaria. Whereas, this presence, may invoke limited indigenous rights, these cannot be seen to have displaced the earlier indigenous rights, and continuous presence of the Jewish People in the area.

Indigenous Peoples

8   While the existence of indigenous peoples was forever a factor in national and international society, only in the past few years did international attention acknowledge that these peoples have rights to their traditional historical and tribal lands, resources, culture, and language that must be recognized and protected by and within the international community.

9   These rights were recently crystallized into the "United Nations Declaration on the Rights of Indigenous People" appended to a United Nations General Assembly Resolution No. 61/295 adopted in 2006. This declaration, generally accepted within the international community, acknowledges the rights of indigenous peoples to their historic lands, territories, and resources, and guarantees their continued rights to maintain and protect these lands, with entitlements to compensation, restitution or redress for lands confiscated or taken.

Today's Political Situation regarding Judea and Samaria

10 The clear and internationally acknowledged historic, indigenous presence of the Jewish People in the Land of Israel including the areas of Judea and Samaria and Jerusalem (historic Palestine) in particular, when placed in the context of today's political situation in the Middle East, and the relationship between Israel and the Palestinians, leads to the following conclusions:

- The indigenous rights of the Jewish people in the areas of Judea and Samaria and Jerusalem (as in Israel itself) are well-founded both historically and legally, and cannot be denied by the international community, whether by individual states or international organizations such as UNESCO.

- These areas cannot, by any account, be termed "occupied territories," which term implies a total lack of historical or legal connection to the area by the Jewish People. This term is also incorrect from the perspective of international law.
- This term together with the term "occupied Palestinian territory," used in UN and international parlance, has no basis whatsoever in law or fact and is nothing more than a non-binding political determination by a political majority of states
- Settlement by Israelis in the areas of Judea and Samaria and Jerusalem (commonly termed, in international parlance "the West Bank"), is not, and cannot be termed as illegitimate, and in any event, cannot be described as an "obstacle to peace in the region." The establishment of towns and villages in the land that is not privately owned by Palestinian residents does not violate any agreement or binding international document.
- Jews have every right to re-establish their residential rights and presence in the area as long as this is done in due deference to existing legally-acquired property rights.
- Any political negotiation aimed at reaching an agreed resolution of the dispute between Israel and the Palestinians cannot disregard the inherent indigenous rights of the Jewish People in the area, in the same way, that it cannot disregard residency and land rights of the

Palestinians in the area. Due deference has to be given by each party to the valid and legitimate historical and legal claims and rights of the other, and this has, in the same manner, to be acknowledged by the international community.

- The United Nations, its member states and major organs, its Secretary-General and all its Specialized Agencies and associated bodies throughout the UN System, all must acknowledge and honor the rights of the indigenous Jewish people in their ancestral home pursuant to the United Nations Declaration on the Rights of Indigenous People. Any action within the various UN organizations on behalf of Palestinian rights at the United Nations must take into consideration the rights of all indigenous people in the region and cannot ignore the indigenous rights of the Jewish People.

Alan Baker

Alan Baker is a former a former ambassador to the State of Israel to Canada and an expert on international law. He also directs the Institute for Contemporary Affairs at the Jerusalem Center for Public Affairs. Baker was one of three members appointed by Prime Minister Benjamin Netanyahu to examine the legal aspects of land ownership pertaining to the West Bank. Chaired by former Justice Edmund Levy, the report, which was published in July 2012, came to be known as the Levy Report.

Indians at Work

Mara Cohen

Courts operate from Canons and Codes of Law. The Supreme Court of the United States operates under and informs us of the Legal interpretation of the US Constitution. Article 6 of the US Constitution establishes a "Special Relationship" between the United States Federal Government and the Indigenous Indian Tribes. Justice Louis Brandeis, the first Jew ever to be appointed as a member of the American Supreme Court, was part of a Jeffersonian tradition that decried "Bigness" [in business and in government; rather, he believed in populism, whether economic or otherwise; that the "small man" in "small communities" has the intellectual capacity to fully participate in the American democratic process by developing his faculties of reason and by educating himself on the issues. He was against big business (corporate monopolies, big banks) and big government—editor.] He appreciated the Tribes' individuality within the broader concept of Individual welfare within political life. The same appreciation he had for Israeli Kibbutzim, and for those who were a part of that movement, he had for US Tribes and their ability to face the challenges of survival as a People.

The following text is a tribute to Justice Brandeis from the news sheet *Indians at Work*, written by John Collier, Commissioner for the Bureau of Indian Affairs, and published by the U.S. Bureau of Indian Affairs, Volume IV, Number 8, December 1, 1936.

"The eightieth birthday of Mr. Justice Louis Brandeis (November 13) should not pass without comment among Indians.

He is one of our great Americans. He is one of a minority race who is wholly faithful to his own people and the more, therefore, not the less, one of our greatest Americans.

Indeed, I venture a further statement. No race or group since ancient Athens has so abstracted its cultural heritage and its peculiar historical genius into expressions valid for the whole world, as has the Jewish race or group. No race or group so holds to its past—coto its spiritual nativity. No race or group so claims modernity for its home. Possibly no race or group may with equal sureness be expected to contribute a distinguishable historical quality to universal man of the far future ages. Among the Jews, Mr. Justice Brandeis is one of the great; and among Americans he is one of the great.

There are three aspects of Mr. Justice Brandeis' philosophy and method which I will mention here, of particular interest to Indians.

One is his profound recognition of the importance of keeping alive, today and hereafter, the significant, energy-building and spiritually orienting group-differences. These group identities and group uniquenesses are the seed-bed and the germplasm of our human world of all future time. Hence, Mr. Justice Brandeis' active devotion to Zionism: hence, his interest in all minorities, and among them the Indians.

Another of the aspects is Mr. Justice Brandeis conviction that humanity's salvation rests in the small things rather than the big things of society: The small independent business; the small cooperative society; the small community-unit; the face-to-face "primary" social group; the team, and the cult, and the guild. For a hundred centuries, the wisest men knew that it was these small-unit facts, not the big facts of empire and of mass combination, which determined one's fate and gave to life its quality. Our generation, excited and overawed by the unstable bignesses which have usurped the world-stage, has tended to belittle or forget the individual and that specific, intimate and unique group activity which is the maker of individuals. Mr. Justice Brandeis is no enemy of bigness, but he is (as a man and as a Supreme Court justice) the active friend of these smaller existences which contain the higher energies of our race. Here, again, Indians peculiarly should be interested in Mr. Justice Brandeis; for their past, and their future too is a small-scale, not a big-scale fact. The small, complexly organized, multiple-interest face-to-face group is, for Indians, undoubtedly the best, even the only possible, institution. Let Indians succeed through it, and their effect upon the world will prove to be out of all proportion to their mere numbers.

Finally, Mr. Justice Brandeis was distinguished as a lawyer through his use of the data and the methods of science. On the Bench, he is a more tireless, and probably a more competent, user of social, economic and human science (including facts statistically measured) than any other Supreme Court justice living or dead. Moreover, this (in the measure that other Justices may emulate it) is a tremendously important item in its bearing upon the future of law and of the court system and the Constitution itself in our country. Indians should take note because it is Indians who today (more systematically, I believe, than any other population or regional groups in America) are trying to do conscious planning based on and tested by experimentation and measurement.

To Mr. Justice Brandeis, many happy birthdays more!"

Uqittuk Mark:
Inuit Defender of Israel

Uqittuk Mark, as told to Machla Abramovitz

My name is Uqittuk Mark, and I've lived my whole life in Ivujivik, an isolated, ice-swept village of 380 people located in the Nunavut region, 2,000 kilometers north of Montreal, Quebec. Ivujivik means "Place where ice accumulates because of strong currents." Situated on a sandy cove sandwiched between imposing cliffs overlooking Hudson Bay and the Hudson Strait, the currents between the two are so strong that the flowing ice often crushes animals living there. In Ivujivik, ice is a constant: There are only three months of the year, from July till October, when there isn't any. No roads link Ivujivik to any other Nunavut villages; the only way into the settlement is by plane. I was born in an igloo, but shortly after my birth, my entire community moved into regular housing. Most young Inuit stay in town; they find jobs here. The majority hunt for a living mainly seals, walrus and beluga. Then, there are those like me who leave temporarily to attend schools of higher education. I studied at the Algonquin College in Ottawa. Today, I work as a weatherman and a control tower operator at the Ijuvik Airport. Our people lived in Ivujivik for 4,000 years.

The Inuit began converting to Anglicanism in the mid-1970s. Along with this conversion came secular knowledge. Before then, we didn't attend school because there were no schools. However, even before that, young people began leaving the traditional ways en masse.

Since attending Sunday school as a young boy, I always longed to visit the Holy Land. I told myself that if the opportunity to go there arises, I will grab it. The opportunity presented itself in 2006 when I joined the Canada Awakening Ministries tour. I was one of 40 participants comprised of First Nations groups, their ministers as well as others from Ireland, Fiji, and Ontario. I was the only male from the North. It was a two-week trip from start to finish, my first outside Canada and it didn't disappoint. For some, it was a life-altering experience: For me, it was a remarkable pilgrimage—a personal journey into the world of the Torah and the New Testament. The stories I learned in Sunday school came alive to me, for instance, the desert where John the Baptist was born and the Sea of Galilee. I felt at home in the Galilee.

We toured most of the land. The only places we didn't visit were the West Bank and Gaza; it was too dangerous to go there. Keeping away from those places, though, didn't immunize us from danger. One kibbutz we visited was hit by Hamas rockets soon after we left. Had we remained longer, we would have been casualties of those missiles, as were many of the Israelis we met there. Seeing and experiencing the land and the people, opened me up to a new perspective on the world and, interestingly, deepened my understanding of what needed to be done to help preserve my own culture.

What struck me most were the differences between Israeli and Canadian culture. In my naiveté, I just assumed that Israel would be yet another Western democracy. I also wasn't prepared for just how traditionally Jewish Israel is. It isn't only the language, the fact that

Israelis speak Hebrew and Yiddish and not English, but I found their customs and traditions unexpected and, at times, inexplicable. In one kibbutz we visited, the kibbutzniks elevated pigs onto a platform; they told us that the Jews weren't allowed to touch them because they were nonkosher. How Israelis observe the Sabbath also intrigued me. There, the Sabbath begins Friday night and ends Saturday night, unlike the Christian Sabbath, which is on Sunday. Orthodox Jews keep the Sabbath according to God's commandment to Moses. For instance, they don't use elevators on the Sabbath: Pushing a knob releases electricity. They consider this work, and Jews aren't allowed to work on the Holy Day.

We also attended museums where we learned Jewish history, especially what happened during the Second World War. Before becoming a state, Jewish settlers weren't allowed to arm themselves; they innovatively bypassed these restrictions. To protect Jews, one man smuggled in guns piece by piece and assembled them in Jerusalem. It was a superhuman effort. I found that awesome.

Israel has much to teach us Inuits about preserving culture. Look at what Eliezer Ben-Yehudah accomplished by reinvigorating the Hebrew language. Ben-Yehuda was a Polish lexicographer and journalist who moved to Palestine in 1881. His accomplishment resonated with me. Over the years, many of us lost our identity, especially after the Canadian government tried assimilating us into the Canadian culture. Besides losing our culture, we also lost our language. In schools, we learned that we should be ashamed of our language. After hearing about what Ben-Yehuda did, I felt encouraged. Perhaps we, too, can reinvigorate our language, albeit with much effort on our parts. Attempts are underway to make that happen. Recently, a few books written in Inuit were published and even a dictionary. More books are sure to follow. I hope all is not yet lost.

Israel has so much more to teach us as a people, especially about how to survive. Jewish history parallels our relationship with a dominant, domineering society. In that regard, we share a deep understanding of what Jews have endured over the centuries and what they continue to endure, even in their own country.

Machla Abramovitz

Machla Abramovitz is a Fellow with the Canadian Institute for Jewish Research and is currently its Publications Editor. She has an M.A, in English Literature from Concordia University and an MLS from McGill University. She's a freelance journalist and author—fiction and nonfiction—who writes for multiple international magazines. Her interests span a variety of subjects including Torah, politics, psychology, physics, and psychology. She's written on all of these subjects.

We have certain expectations of native people. They have to be militant. They should be political radicals, and quick to rebuke white people, the "colonizers." They should bang on drums, chanting in a tongue that no one else can understand, and refer to the mysteries of the Great Spirit.

Very often, native people know what's expected of them, and if in the mood, will play the role. My friend Uqittuk Mark won't. He refuses to be the aggrieved Aboriginal. When I first visited his community in the early 1980s, he didn't lecture me about the evils of the white man.

Instead, he pulled out his guitar and gave me a folk music concert, with songs by Pete Seeger, Bob Dylan, and more. We did discuss native issues, but not as personal accusations. Instead, we talked to improve our understanding. Uqittuk's critiques of government policy on education and development were passionate but even-handed.

When I recently reconnected with Uqittuk, he again greeted me with the same warm demeanor as I experienced decades ago. He still takes the issues affecting his family and community quite seriously, and he still uses the approach of trying to achieve understanding.

A significant change is that he is now a committed Christian. He is passionate about his beliefs, and in keeping with his character, Uquittuk is always trying to understand more. He told me about his recent Israel pilgrimage, which had a profound spiritual effect on him.

Uqittuk is a kind of sandwich generation of Inuit. Their modern education limited their ability to learn traditional hunting. The influence of western popular culture affected them, whether in music, food, or livelihood. Uqittuk and I had many discussions about authenticity: Was his generation authentically Inuit? Was my generation authentically Jewish? They're not "real" Inuit, he and his friends declared, because they were educated in accordance with someone else's culture. It took a few years, but I eventually realized his perspective was right, and mine wrong. And not just about the Inuit.

Uqittuk is authentic: as an Inuk (Eskimo), Christian, and as a sensitive and intelligent friend. It's an honor to have him offer to tell CIJR about his Israel pilgrimage.

Nathan Elberg

Jews, *Conversos*, and Native Americans: The Iberian Experience

Jose Faur

Sir: I am Jewish and profess the Law of Moses, and by it, I shall live and die. And if I would have to swear, I shall swear by the living God, who made heaven and earth and is the God of Israel.
—Francisco Maldonado de Silva. Martyr, 1627
　First Argentine Martyr in the battle against Spanish Oppression[1]

The Spaniards in Mexico and Peru used to baptize Indian infants and then immediately dash their brains out: by this means they secured that these infants went to Heaven.
—Bertrand Russell[2]

Having been raised in Buenos Aires, I believe that the fate of Jews, *Conversos* (Christians with even partial Jewish background), and Native Americans are closely knitted: all were victims of Spanish persecution. As a Jew, the story of the *Converso* cannot be closed. Our tradition maintains that something special in their manners and outlook has endured. Throughout the Americas, throughout the Southwest of the U.S.A., there are groups of people actively investigating their family roots. Some visit Israel. Others try to establish a rapport with local Jewish communities. It is also high time for the Jewish communities to enter into a dialogue with Native American communities. There is much that can be learned from each other's experiences. We are both survivors of the same type of horrendous holocaust, ignited by greed, malice, and intolerance. In this sense, one may ascertain that the natives, too, are brothers from the Ten Lost Tribes of Israel.

The underlying theory of this study is that Visigothic military ideology (dominating European aristocracy until modern days) was the principal factor in the persecution and extermination of Jewish life in Spain. This ideology has nothing to do with religion. Rather, it pertains to the dark side of humankind: the manipulation of religion (or other ideologies) for cynical purposes. In the Iberian case, it consisted in the transformation of the *cristiano viejo* (Iberian Christian into a *Conquistador*, a superior being encrusted in iron, mercilessly destroying the "other;" first Jews, then *Conversos*, and later Native Americans. The expulsion of Jews from Spain unfolded into the Expulsion of Spain from the rest of Europe. Under the pretext of orthodoxy, the Spanish Crown, in particular with Philip II on, isolated Spain from the rest of Europe. Spain is the only nation in Western Europe that did not have a Renaissance. In the end, what divided the *cristiano viejo* from the Jew was, precisely what divided the *cristiano viejo* from other Europeans.

Historians on behalf of Spanish inhumanity tell us that the racist persecutions were "necessary" in order to attain national unity. It is a lie, backed up by neither reasoned argument nor evidence. The whole notion of "national unity" was alien to the Spanish mind. The Spanish language does not even have a word for "Spaniard;" *Español* is a Provencal term.[3] Whatever unity prevailed in Spain was the result of a strong central government, not of a "national conscience." Even today,

Spain continues to be the most divided country in Europe: linguistically, socially, culturally, politically, and religiously.

The main argument of this study is that the same people that persecuted Jews and Conversos committed the greatest genocide in human history: the almost total extermination of the native population of Latin America. Whatever "reasons" concocted by historians to "explain" Spanish policies against Jews and Conversos cannot possibly apply to Spanish treatment of Native Americans. Apologists for Spanish inhumanity argue that many native Americans were devastated by plagues. The argument is essentially racist. It uncritically assumes that the native's immunity system was biologically inferior and unable to cope with the white's man superior viruses and bacteria. There is no evidence for such a view. Somehow, we are expected to believe that the natives' immunity system failed only when in contact with Spaniards, but it could work fine when confronting non-Iberians, or Iberians with a Jewish background, the Conversos. Or that these viruses failed to do their macabre work in places that were not rich in gold and silver, like Argentina. Finally, we are expected to believe that Spanish viruses were sensitive to cost and productivity and therefore inactive with the black slaves imported as substitutes for native American. It is by examining Spanish policies in Spain and the New World as a single phenomenon—rather than as two disconnected events that the monstrous nature of Spanish persecutions can be gauged.

A few words about the methodology used in this study. Invariably, Western historiography espouses the perspective of the persecutor. The objective of the historian is to simultaneously express the view of the persecutor and discredit the historical memory of the persecuted, even when expressing empathy for the victims. The view of this author is that Jewish historiography must express the perspective of the persecuted.[4] As such, the major objective here is to project the events from the perspective of the victims: the Jews, the Conversos, and Native Americans.

The Conceptual Bases of Greed

Greed is a concept peculiar to Visigothic military ideology that was further implanted in the *cristiano viejo*.[5] It includes two elements: coveting of wealth and contempt for labor. Reflecting the military-aristocratic ideal that might is right, the *cristiano viejo* came to believe that wealth is to be acquired by plundering somebody else's toil. Labor is demeaning: it contradicts the ideal of *honor* (honor) and *honra* (dignity). In this essential point, the *cristiano viejo* differed from the *cristiano nuevo*. The new Christian, from his Jewish past, believed in the sanctity of labor. He also espoused that wealth is to be acquired by diligence and industry. These were subversive ideas. They denied the hierarchical structure of society, whereby the inferior owe unconditional obedience to the superior—in our case, represented by the military or ecclesiastical aristocracy—precisely because the latter was *superior* and the former was *inferior*.[6] The idea that an individual could climb up above a particular group, as proposed by the *Converso*, stood in flagrant contradiction to the corporational view of humanity, borrowed by Christianity from Roman *corporatio*. As with the old tribal ideology, the corporational ideal demands that people never be viewed as individuals.[7] The ideal of individuality proposed by the *cristiano nuevo* threatened the very foundation of Spanish society.

The preceding is essential to understand the system of castes (*castas*) upon which Spanish society rested. Américo Castro (1885–1972) was the first scholar to note that Spanish society is structured on the basis of "[c]astes, rather than [c]lasses."[8] Class is radically different than cast:

The social class bases its rank on what it does; the rank of the caste depends on the mere existence of the person: in the last analysis, all the Hispano-Christians ended up feeling themselves a superior caste by virtue of the fact that they were Christians and not Moors or Jews.[9]

It is a thoroughly racist term. The lowliest *cristiano viejo* felt superior to a *Cristiano nuevo* simply because he belonged to a higher cast of people: a superior race.[10]

Historians struggle to explain the "two Spains" phenomena: one enlightened and progressive, the other reactionary and brutal; one concerned with life and living, the other, obsessed with mortality. In fact, these "Spains" are the effect of two mutually exclusive ideologies. The slaughtering of Jewish and *conversos* communities throughout Spain, the establishment of the Inquisition, and the Expulsion in 1492 represent the attempt of one Spain to strangulate the other. Invariably, the strategy of the *cristiano viejo* consisted in eliminating, rather than confronting divergence. In the final account, whereas Jews and *conversos* created the "golden age" of Spanish letters and sciences,[11] *cristianos viejos* created "the age of gold:" a civilization dominated by rapacity. This constituted the sole basis of Spanish policy in the Americas.

The Policy of Greed

The key is greed. Because work offended Spanish *honra*, the *conquistador* was not interested in developing the territories coming under his domain. The sole purpose for his coming to the New World was to acquire *honra*, the acquisition of wealth *without* labor. Even the most basic forms of labor, such as cultivating the land or drawing water, was repulsive for the *cristiano viejo*. In 1590, the early settlers of Buenos

Aires addressed a complaint to Philip II protesting that since the natives refused to work, they "had to plow and dig with our own hands."[12]

For the Spaniards, America represented the possibility of accumulating precious metals *without* toil. Hence, "the utopian ideology," the search for *el Dorado*, and other similar reveries characterizing the *conquistador*'s mind.[13] Unlike the English and Dutch, who worked and developed the land, the *conquistador* did not view the territories as a new home, but as a place containing fabulous mines to be extracted and transported *quickly* away to the Iberian Peninsula. This attitude prohibited striking roots in the new land. As a conqueror—and this is the precise sense in which the term *conquistador* ought to be understood—the right of the Spaniard rested on the facts created on the ground by his sword. Therefore he felt no responsibility either to the land or its original inhabitants. Since his sole objective was to transport the wealth of America to the Iberian Peninsula, those places that were not rich in precious metals were of no interest.

A point in case is Argentina, poor in precious metals but fabulously wealthy in land for agriculture and grazing. Significantly, there is no record of even a single Spaniard with a title of nobility settling in that country. During the colonial period, there was practically no government. Disappointed at not finding rich minerals, Spain neglected the land. According to a report from 1770, the streets of Buenos Aires were impassable during the rain. As late as 1852, the city that would be known as the "Paris of Latin America" was a pest-ridden village. The enormous economic and intellectual progress later made by Argentina was possible *precisely* because it had been neglected by the Spanish Crown.

The consequences of the Spanish policy on the economic and political history of both Europe and the Americas will be examined next.

The Devil Is Always the Other

The ethical basis of greed is to be found in the Western idea of the "other," an alien bereft of the most basic rights. To the Indo-European mind—"the dogs which followed the camp had more in common with it than the tribesmen of an alien and unrelated tribe."[14] Linguistically and psychologically, the alien was identified with "the enemy."[15] During the Middle Ages, Europe witnessed the emergence of persecuting societies, containing a distinct group—women, lepers, Jews, heretics, etc.—marked for persecution.[16] It was axiomatic that morality did *not* apply to the "other." In the eyes of the Church, "love" does not apply to members of other religions. Christianity was the first religious system (followed by Islam) to introduce the idea of a religious enemy whereby all non-Christians are regarded as sub-humans and bereft of rights.[17] According to Christian doctrine, Jews had the legal status of slaves. Consequently, there could not be a moral objection to plunder and despoil them from their property. This doctrine was enunciated with candor and precision by Thomas Aquinas, who wrote: "Since Jews are the slaves of the Church, the Church may take disposition of their property."[18]

Spanish historians insist that Spanish persecution was neither racist nor anti-Semitic, but simply a matter of national unity to be accomplished through religion. It takes a certain level of mental turpitude not to realize that the slaughtering of new Christians, the promulgation of the infamous edicts of *pureza de sangre*, barring Christians with even partial Jewish ancestry from occupying a civil or ecclesiastical office, the hatred and contempt that *cristianos viejos* projected toward their new co-religionists, had nothing to do with "religion." Thus, Spain inaugurated a series of racial persecutions to be paralleled only several centuries later by the infamous Nuremberg legislation.[19]

"Christian religion" was an excuse to justify Spanish rapacity. No lesser a political analyst than Machiavelli (1469–1527) concluded that "religion" was but a subterfuge for rapacity.

Historians have labored assiduously to explain Spanish treatment of Jews and *conversos* on the basis of religious, political, or economic considerations. One of them reasoned:

> [A]ll civilizations move towards their destiny, whether willingly or unwillingly. If the train in which I am sitting moves off, the passenger in a train alongside has the sensation of moving in opposite direction . . . Spain was moving towards a political unity, which could not be conceived, in the sixteenth century, as anything other than religious unity. Israel meanwhile was being carried towards the destiny of the *diaspora* . . . Even as lucid an observer as Francisco Quevedo saw it possessing diabolical features. The devil is always the Other.[20]

This spurious explanation is an irresponsible justification of every atrocity performed by a civilization on her path towards her "destiny"—including the Nazi "final solution." It was malice—pure and unadulterated—that moved Spain.

The same Spaniards who persecuted Jews and *Conversos* hounded Native Americans savagely, although none of the alleged reasons applied. De Proodian justifies the racist legislation prohibiting Christians with even partial Jewish ancestry to immigrate to America, with the following instruction issued to Columbus:

> That it should be attempted to convert the Indians to the [Catholic] faith . . . In order that the Indians should love our religion, they should be treated lovingly and should be given some merchandise and gifts of ours.

According to de Proodian, the presence of Christians with even partial Jewish blood would have interfered with the labor of love and kindness that only *cristianos viejos* could properly perform. Therefore, their presence had to be barred from the New World.[21]

It is instructive to see how this labor of love was carried on. Pedro Mártir (1459–1525) wrote:

> In the midst of such an abundant plenty, there is something that gives me no small anguish. These men, so simple and naked, were used to work little; now many perish as a result of the great exhaustion in the mines, and they are desperate to the point that many kill themselves and do not care to raise children. They tell that the pregnant mothers take medicine to abort, seeing that they would give birth to slaves for the Christians ... The number of these wretched had diminished immensely; many say that once was made a census of one million two hundred thousand, how many there is today, it causes me a horror to say.[22]

Not a single soul of the native population of Jamaica, Bermuda, St. Thomas, Puerto Rico, Panama, Cuba, etc., survived. Todorov had shown that in the course of only fifty years, the Iberian conquerors reduced the population of Native Americans from eighty million to ten million. By the year 1600, the original population of Mexico was reduced from twenty-five million to one million. This is the greatest genocide in recorded history, in absolute and relative terms.[23] None of the "explanations" justifying Spanish persecution of Jews could possibly apply to native Americans. In terms of religion, they were totally submissive and willing fully to accept the teachings of the Church. Nor did they pose a threat that could possibly compromise Spanish "national, unity." On the contrary, they were politically stable and constituted an invaluable economic asset to the Crown. And yet, even the darkest periods of history witnessed nothing comparing the Spanish atrocities against Native Americans.

Consider the common practice of snatching children from their mother's arms and throwing them to be devoured alive by dogs, or smashing them against the rocks and throwing them to die in the mountains. The usual way to kill native leaders was in groups of thirteen, in honor of Jesus and the twelve apostles! The Spanish sexual mores deserve special attention. When a young Native American wife explained to a Spanish captain that she could not have sex with him because she had promised her husband to be faithful, the captain unleashed the dogs and had them devour her alive.[24] It was common for the Spaniards to take not only the properties of these wretched [native Americans], but also their daughters, taking them by force and rape them; if they do not give consent of their own will, they tie them, and torture them, lash them and punish them with great cruelty . . . Their [native American] women if they would find out that someone had had relations with her [native Americans] husband, they burn them, mistreat and torture them, lash them and bring them before their eyes in irons, stripped, exposed, abused, dog-bitten and very hurt.[25]

On June 4, 1559, Fernando de Santillan (sixteenth century) reported how the Spaniards in Chile "unleashed their dogs against some [native Americans], burnt others, in addition to mutilating them, cutting their noses, arms, or breasts, and invented a thousand other ways to tear them into pieces."[26] It was customary that for reasons of work distribution, a few Spaniards would parcel a native family among themselves. Thus, one would take the wife, another would take the husband, and a third the children, "in the same manner as if they would have been pigs."[27] In addition to those dying of sickness, exhaustion, ill-treatment, and abuse, we must consider those who simply "were buried alive in the mines."[28]

So much for acts of loving kindness.

The crimes perpetrated by the Spaniards against Jews and *conversos* came from the same source that contrived the crimes against Native Americans: they were crimes against humanity. To "explain" those crimes is to excuse evil and renounce morality. With their convoluted "reasons," modern historians join the persecutors. Theirs is historiography of the persecutor whereby the Devil is always the Other.

The Victims of Greed

The parallels between the fate of Jews and *conversos* and Native Americans go further. In both cases, the official pretext for persecution were bulls issued by "political popes." In the case of the Jews, it was a bull issued in 1478 by Sixtus IV (1471–1484), the basis for the establishment of the Inquisition in 1481. In the case of Native Americans, it was Alexander VI (1492–1503, awarding the Spanish Crown the exclusive right to bring Christianity to the New World. In both cases, the bulls served as an excuse to simultaneously despoil and demonize the victim under the pretext of "religion."

In the case of Native Americans, it was debated whether they were indeed humans or beasts. Pope Paul III in 1537 issued a decision ascertaining that Native Americans do have a "soul." The decision served two purposes. It absolved the Spaniards from the sin of bestiality and legitimized their oppressive behavior, as it required bringing Native Americans into the fold.

Christianity, it has been noted, has produced not only the largest number of saints but also the largest number of fanatics. Under the excuse of "religion," Spanish priests committed some of the most heinous atrocities. In the Americas, Spanish missionaries justified their sadistic impulses in the name of "religion." On the basis of the inerrant doctrine that "whoever loves you well will make you cry" Christian priests unleashed their brutal force against Native Americans. All that the natives need "is bread and whipping." Priests had their own jails and instruments of torture to bring the natives close to the religion of love. Their abuses were scandalous even by Spanish standards. King Philip II had to issue an order in 1570 restraining them.[29] Priests, known for their promiscuity, used their position to increase their *honra* by further despoiling the natives. Their behavior became so outrageous that the Church was forced to investigate.[30]

Slander is used by persecuting societies to justify their treatment of the "other." In Spain there circulated series of libelous accusations designed to dehumanize the Jew and justify anti-Jewish atrocities. "There isn't an evil so atrocious or a cruelty so vile," wrote Isaac Cardoso, "that they have not imputed it to them."[31] These are psychological projections, whereby the persecutor projects onto the victim precisely those impulses that he must suppress.[32] Native Americans, too, were slandered in order to justify Spanish atrocities. De Oviedo (1478–1557) justified Spaniards taking the gold from the natives, "since is better that it should be in the hands of men and not of beasts."[33] The Spaniards' view was that natives are so evil they "commit suicide just to impoverish the Spaniards with their death." They deserved to be exterminated as a divine punishment for their many vices.[34]

The accusations represent psychological rather than moral concern. Consider the charge that the natives were guilty of idolatry. The worship of images is an issue that had divided Christianity throughout the ages. It emerged again, in the fifteenth century as a result of the ingression of *conversos* in the Church. By the sixteenth century, it was voiced by enlightened Christians, moved by the new spirit of humanism and reform, and not only by Jews and *conversos*. The principal point was that there are no objective grounds by which "the worship of idols" can be distinguished from "the adoration of images." (Thus, whatever theological argument could justify the worship or adoration of images in the Christian Church could justify the worship or adoration of images among Native Americans).[35] Only when analyzed on psychological grounds, as a typical case of repression and projection, does the charge of "idolatry" make sense: by projecting the guilt onto the victim, the persecutor absolves himself of sin.

The same applies to the accusation that natives practiced human sacrifice, an accusation based on fact. But Spaniards were guilty of the same crime. What is the incineration of old and young, men and women, *Autos de Fe*—"acts of faith"—but human sacrifices on behalf of Christianity? What about the slaughtering of Native Americans? Wasn't this a veritable form of human sacrifice? Is there any other way to classify the killing of Native American leaders in groups of thirteen, in honor of Jesus and the twelve apostles? The same psychological mechanism underlies the Spanish condemnation of natives' sexual mores. It is worth noting that the early Spanish chronicles saw nothing offensive in the sexual life of the natives. It is only *after* they committed sexual crimes against the natives that the Spaniards accused them of sexual crimes.

Imperial Economy

There is a further parallel. Traditionally, the Visigothic economy depends on the exploitation of a minority: first Jews, then *Conversos* (and Moors), and finally native Americans. Without these elements, Spain would have collapsed.[36] During the period of the *Reconquistei*, the Spanish economy depended on the services provided by the Jews as tax-farmers, businessmen, artisans, scientists, and diplomats. The very day that the *Reconquista* finished, the Catholic Monarchs announced the Expulsion of Jews. By August 3, 1492, every professing Jew had to leave Spain. Henceforth, the Spanish economy would depend on two segments of the population, *Conversos*, and Moors. Shortly thereafter, Spain developed an "imperial economy," a dimension of Visigothic greed. Hard currency enables its possessor to acquire wealth with *honra*, that is, without labor. Since the new territories awarded Spain unlimited access to precious metals and minted of money, there was no need for financial planning and management. *Conversos* (for business and financial organization) and Moors (for basic labor, agriculture, and industry) were now expendable. Charles V's savage persecution of Moors and *Conversos* underlines the structural relationship between the imperial economy and the racist policies. In 1522, he issued the infamous order prohibiting Christians with even partial Jewish or Moorish ancestry from entering America.[37] Just as the sword had rendered the *cristiano viejo* invincible in the battlefield, precious metals will render him financially invincible.

The (mis-)management of enormous monetary wealth became the cornerstone of Philip II's administration. He had been properly described as "a merciless bigot," known for his promiscuity. He devoted his life to implementing his father's policy, the biggest economic fiasco in the annals of history. In addition to the physical and cultural genocide of millions and millions of innocents, this policy was responsible for squandering the largest amount of gold and silver known to man. It reduced Spain to spiritual and economic desolation. It also proved conclusively Spain's utter incompetence and its parasitic structure.

Jews had been a major factor in the economy of the country. Their expulsion in 1492 and the subsequent persecution of *cristianos nuevos* produced a vacuum that needed urgently to be filled. Since all forms of industry and commerce deeply offended the *honra*, the vacuum was filled by importing the most basic goods. Foreign artisans, merchants, and bankers were now replacing the Jew. Goods were imported at exorbitant prices. The new Spanish administrators were not only inexperienced but also corrupt. In a short time, the entire economy was controlled by foreign interests. The imperial economy of Spain consisted in paying for all its need with the gold and silver extracted from America with forced labor. Without these metals, Spain could not have paid even for its most basic necessities. But the payment of debts in hard cash is not a simple matter. Pirates and bandits made the transportation of cash and precious metals costly, fraught with danger.[38] Spanish investments in Europe crumbled. In 1556, King Philip II was forced to declare bankruptcy. The Crown declared bankruptcy again in 1557, 1560, 1575, 1596, 1607, and 1627.[39] Since there were neither Jew nor *Converso* to plunder, public funds were plundered.[40] There was a last ditch effort to revamp the economy, made by the *Conde-Duque* de Olivares with the help of Portuguese *Conversos*. He was censured for these efforts. de Olivares was censured for counting in his entourage bankers who "under a disguise" concealed their "circumcision." de Olivares was the author of a work addressed to the king, in which he chastised the *cristiano viejo* establishment for their disastrous policies.[41] He was henceforth dismissed by the king and denounced to the Inquisition. If not for the fact that he soon died, he would have ended in the Inquisition's cell.[42] The *cristiano viejo* would rather be ruined than helped by someone with Jewish ancestry.[43]

Eventually, all the wealth of Spain ended up in the purses of foreign nations. Spain became "a mere channel for silver from its colonies."[44] It was a secondary detail in the passing of the treasures from America to Europe.

Thus, in a supreme act of justice, the wealth that had been plundered from Jews, *Conversos*, and Native Americans was in turn plundered from the Spaniards by foreign merchants and bankers, as well as by pirates and bandits. The precious metals that they took away from America ended in the vaults of other European capitals—not in Toledo, Seville, and Madrid.

Jews, *Conversos*, and Native Americans were the victims of the same diabolical forces. Their destruction was justified with theological reasons. The argument was made that in their destruction the natives were serving the white race so that their existence acquired meaning. They could now die happily, knowing that their destruction served the sustenance of the superior. The argument acquires unfailing logic when assuming the hierarchical view of humanity peculiar to Christianity:

> The white race and the Indian race are like two sisters that their father wanted to marry off. The first one is very beautiful and intelligent; her marriage presents no difficulties since she does not lack suitors. But the other is very ugly, lazy, stupid, and dumb. In order to get married, she would need a valuable dowry, a rich trousseau, and also something else. The dowry of the ugly daughter is the precious metals in the American soil.[45]

The Spanish Exception to the Conquistador

A determining factor in the Jewish attitude towards Native Americans is the Jewish view of the "other." In Hebrew tradition, the "other" is not a "deformed" being, but only a different expression of the "image of God," common to the children of Adam, the father of *all* humanity. The Hebrew term *kamokha*, "as yourself;" connotes a horizontal perspective. The biblical commandment to "love the other as yourself (*kamokha*)" excludes a vertical perception of the "other," with all the monstrous consequences that this commandment had in the Christian tradition.[46] This is evident in the first encounter between Jews and Native Americans. They viewed them not as inferior beings but as members of the Ten Lost Tribes. Although historically incorrect,[47] their view expressed the basic semantic orientation peculiar to Hebrew humanistic tradition: those who are different are ancient brothers.[48]

Apologists for Spanish inhumanity point to the few voices raised in indignation against the Spaniards' atrocities. The most prominent was Bartalorne de Las Casas, the great champion of Native American rights. But he was not a *cristiano viejo*; Las Casas was indeed a *Converso*. For defending the rights of Native Americans he was branded "the enemy of Spain."[49]

When Las Casas ordered the members of the order of the Hieronymites to free the natives, they simply refused to obey him. When he denounced them for the extermination of the entire population of Lucayas, Las Casas was in danger.[50] The Hieronymites joined with the *Conquistadores* to have him expelled. Las Casas had to return to Spain. In 1550, Philip II assigned his position to another bishop.[51] Antonio de Guevara, the writer who brought to light the plight of Native Americans, also came from a converso background, as did other advocates for the natives.[52]

There is another difference between the attitude of the *Conquistador*, and that of the Jew and *Converso*. The *cristiano viejo* "lacked the tradition and habit of work, of being socially productive."[53] The reason that Spain refused to participate in the intellectual and scientific progress taking place in Europe was that in Spain almost all the philosophical and scientific works had been produced by Jews and *Conversos*. Since the *cristianos viejos* viewed the other in purely racist terms, they "regarded intellectual activities as proper to Jews alone."[54] They could not participate in any scientific or productive enterprise, for "the terror of being taken for a Jew. This was the reason for the cultural backwardness of the Spaniards."[55]

The new Christians and Jews arriving at the New World did not come to accumulate the maximum amount of precious metals and run back to the Iberian Peninsula. Rather, like the British and the Dutch, their main objective was to *develop* the land and make it their home.

The bigoted policies of Philip II were intended to prevent such people from settling in the Americas. The persecutions intensified. Law IX issued the following order to the Spanish American colonies: "That they should try to clean the land of Foreigners and people who are suspect in matters of Faith."

A decree issued in 1602, reads:

> We order that the Viceroys, Audiences, and governors, and charge the Archbishops and Bishops, that they should . . . try to clean the land from that people, and make them be expelled from the Indias, and ship them in the first opportunity at their own expense, and be extremely diligent to inform us.[56]

Because of its more liberal policies, many Jews and Conversos had settled in Brazil. With the fall of the Dutch government in 1654, they scattered all over the Americas. Some, like those who settled in Argentina, became the founders of the most distinguished families of the country.[57] Like their brothers in North America, these men fought on the side of the people for freedom.

Spanish credibility was nil. The Argentine people continued with their revolution, which spread to the rest of Latin America. The revolutionary Simon Bolivar was particularly helped by the Jewish community. After a major defeat, he took refuge in the house of a Jew, to whom he was extremely grateful.

In 1846, a petition was addressed to Don Pedro Santana, the first President of the Dominican Republic requesting that measures be taken against four or five Jews who were interfering with the cartel organized by local merchants. President Santana confronted this outrage. His reply is both a manifesto against Spanish racism and a defense of Jewish and *Converso* humanism. He attacked the greedy monopolists who were "exploiting the wretched peasants whom they sacrifice." Instead of trying to expel the Jews, they should emulate their industry and productivity. The use of religious prejudice to rob innocent people of their basic rights is an affront to religion: "[To] persecute a peaceful man and prevent him from buying tobacco under the pretext of religion is an outrageous abuse of Christian doctrine."

He declared that Jews are genuine patriots, an asset to the nation, who deserve praise. In fact, they were the first to contribute to the freedom of the country. It would be a travesty of justice if people like them would be denied the basic rights that the Constitution guarantees to all.

Jews are also an asset to society. Far from being a threat to other religions, they are a benefit even to religious institutions not their own. Jews seek freedom from religious subjection and the right to practice their own religion without outside interference. That is why not only do they not impose their religion on others or try to gain proselytes, but they respect other religions and help with their alms.

To Jews and Conversos, these words sound with special resonance: they are a fulfillment of their long struggle for freedom. It is as if President Santana, z"l, stretched out a consoling hand: redeeming with grace and compassion the tears of those who endured so much pain and ignominy for their vision of freedom.

José Faur

José Faur was born and raised in Buenos Aires, Argentina and belonged to the Damascene Syrian Jewish community of that city. He was tutored in Jewish subjects by several Sepharadi Rabbis specially hired by his parents to this end. Hakham Eliahu Freue, cited by Faur as his principal teacher, was the spiritual head of the Damascus community in Argentina and taught Faur the fundamentals of Talmud, Jewish law and rabbinics. He later attended Beth Medrash Govoha in Lakewood, New Jersey, followed by studies in Semitic Philology and linguistics at the University of Barcelona. He accepted a faculty position at the Jewish Theological Seminary of America, but later resigned, and sued the institution over their acceptance of women. He taught at the Spertus Institute in Chicago, Bar Ilan University, and Netanya Academic College. He has published many original and insightful books, such as *The Horizontal Society. Understanding the Covenant and Alphabetic Judaism*, and *Homo Mysticus. A Guide to Maimonides's Guide for the Perplexed*. He has written many articles, published in Spanish, English and Hebrew.

1   There is a novel on his life and ideas, by Marcos Aguinis, *La Gesta del Marrano* (Buenos Aires: Planeta, 1993). Unless otherwise stipulated, all translations in the following are mine.
2   Bertrand Russell, *Why I Am Not a Christian* (New York: Simon and Schuster, 1957), p. 35.

3   Américo Castro, *La realidad histórica de España* (Mexico: Editorial Porrúa, 1982), p. 18.
4   See my *In the Shadow of History* (New York: SUNY, 1992), pp. 189–193.
5   Particularly Castile, incarnating Visigothic ideology to the present, but not necessarily those of Catalonia and Andalusia.
6   *In the Shadow of History*, pp. 3–33.
7   Ibid., pp. 28–29.
8   Américo Castro, *The Structure of Spanish History*, trans. Edmund L. King (Princeton: Princeton University Press, 1954), p. 607.
9   Ibid., p. 609.
10 *The Structure of Spanish History*, pp. 611, 612. Cr, below, ns. 78–79.
11 *In the Shadow of History*, pp. 29–32, and chaps. 4–6.
12 Cited in ibid., p. 57. Cf., Fernand Braudel, *Capitalism and Material Life 1400–1800*, trans. Miriam Kochan (New York: Harper Colophon Books, 1973), p. 407.
13 *La peculiaridad linguistica rioplatense*, pp. 45, 47.
14 Sir Henry Sumner Maine, *The Early History of Institutions* (Port Washington: Kennikat Press, 1966), p. 65.
15 *In the Shadow of History*, pp. 4–8.
16 R.I. Moore, *The Formation of the Persecuting Society* (Oxford: Basil Blackwell, 1987); and *In the Shadow of History*, pp. 1–2.
17 *In the Shadow of History*, p. 198.
18 *Summa Theologica* II, 2, 10, 10. Cited in *The Structure of Spanish History*, p. 471, n. 10, in the name of Rosa Lida. Since the original could prove a bit unsettling, the English version in ed. Timothy McDermot, *Summa Theologicae* (London: Eyre and Spottiswoode, 1989), p. 341, was rendered: "The church has the right to dispose of the Jew's property since he is the subject of the church."
19 *In the Shadow of History*, p. 232, n. 12. Cf., ibid., pp. 233–234, n. 41.
20 Ibid., p. 825; cf., ibid., pp. 823–826.
21 *Los judios en America*, p. 22.
22 Pedro Mártir de Anglería, *Libros de las dicadas del Nuevo Mundo* (Buenos Aires:

Editorial Bajel, 1944), Dec. III, Lib. VIII, chap. I, p. 273.

23 Tzvetan Todorov, *La conquête de l'Amérique* (Paris: Éditions du Seuil, 1982), pp. 138–139.

24 *In the Shadow of History*, pp. 4–5.

25 Quoted in Henry Méchoulan, *El honor de Dios* (Barcelona: Editorial Argos Vergara, 1981), p. 49

26 Quoted in ibid., p. 41.

27 Quoted in ibid., p. 51.

28 Quoted in ibid., p. 53.

29 *El honor de Dios*, p. 43.

30 Ibid., pp. 44–45.

31 *Las Excelencias de los Hebreos* (Amsterdam, 1679), p. 408.

32 *In the Shadow of History*, pp. 209–210.

33 Cited in Alberto M. Salas, *Tres cronistas de Indias* (Mexico: Fondo de Cultura Económica, 1959), p. 119.

34 Ibid., p. 120.

35 On the worship of images in Christianity, see Edwyn Bevan, *Holy Images* (London, 1940). On the input of the conversos in this debate, see *In the Shadow of History*, p. 40. For the converso charge against cristianos viejos of the crime of idolatry, see *Los judios en America*, p. 148.

36 Moorish conquest and subsequent domination of the Iberian Peninsula was possible because Visigothic Spain lacked an effective economic structure. As Américo Castro had shown, even after the Reconquista the working class in Spain were the Moors (they were the ones who actually cultivated the land, a people "who would not let a single space of land go to waste"), and the merchants were the Jews. The policy of the Spanish central government was to exploit its productive minorities. In modern times, when there no longer were Jews, Moors, or native Americans to be exploited, Spanish policy had been to exploit the Catalonian population. This had been the most productive (and hence the least antisemitic segment of Spain). Their love and capacity for in-

dustry and labor had been captured in a Sephardic proverb, "Los Catalans—de las Piedras sacan panes" ("The Catalonians can extract bread from stones"). Hence the tension characterizing the relations between the central government of Spain and Catalonians (and other productive minorities).

37 *Los judíos en America*, p. 20.
38 On the problems connected with the transference and payment of hard currency, see *The Mediterranean and the Mediterranean World in the Age of Philip II*, vol. 1, pp. 476–508.
39 Ibid., vol. 1, pp. 505–517; vol. 2, pp. 897, 960–966.
40 Ibid., pp. 506–517; 897–900.
41 On the nature and character of the "grimdes" and other members of the nobility, see ibid., pp. 709–718.
42 For a general view of his life and accomplishments, see Gregorio Marañon, *El Conde-Duque de Olivares* (Madrid: Espasa-Calpe, 1962).
43 *El honor de Dios*, pp. 142–148.
44 *Capitalism and Material Life 1400–1800*, p. 345.
45 Quoted in *El honor de Dios*, p. 39.
46 *In the Shadow of History*, pp. 6–7, and p. 220, n. 19. Semantically, the Hebrew re'akha, usually translated "friend," actually means "other."
47 Elberg-Schwartz article in this volume-Ed.
48 Ibid., p. 7.
49 Américo Castro, "Fray Bartolomé de las Casas o Casaus," in *Cervantes y los casticismos españoles* (Madrid: Alianza Editorial, 1974), pp. 73–74; and the monograph by Marcel Bataillon and Andre Saint-Lu, *Las Casas et la défense des Indiens* (Paris: Julliard, 1971).
50 See Fray Antonio de Remesal, *Historia general de las Indias Occidentales* (Guatemala: Tip. Nacional, 1932), vol. 1, p. 177.
51 The best overview of Las Casas' views and activities, from which many of the references of this work proceed, is *Tres cronistas de Indias*, pp. 161–301.
52 On his family background, see Stephen Gilman, "The Sequel to El Villano del

Danubio," in *Revista Hispánica Moderna*, 51 (1965), pp. 177–185. On his life and accomplishment, see Augustin Redondo, *Antonio de Guevara (1480–1545) et l'Espagne de son temps* (Geneva: Librairie Droz, 1976).

53 *De la edad conflictiva*, p. 91.
54 *La Realidad Historica de Espana*, p. xxiv.
55 *De la edad conflictiva*, p. 118.
56 *Documentos de Historia Americana*, p. 70.
57 Mario Javier Saban, *Judlos Conversos: Los antepasados judios de las familias tradicionales argentinas* (Buenos Aires: Distal, 1990). For some interesting details in the lives of these early settlers, see Matilde Gini de Barnatan, "Los Criptos Judios del Rio de la Plata en el siglo XVI," in Abraham Haim, ed., *Society and Community* (Jerusalem: Misgav Yerushalayim, 1991), pp. 103–118.

Select Bibliography

Abruzzi, William S. "Colonialization and Resistance in North America and Palestine: Similar Historical Processes." 2003. http://www.drabruzzi.com/iindians_and_palestinian.htm

Aloni, Yossi. "Two More Native American Chiefs Pledge Support to Israel." *Israel Today*, March 11, 2013. http://www.israeltoday.co.il/NewsItem/tabid/178/nid/23722/Default.aspx

Avineri, Shlomo. *The Making of Modern Zionism. The Intellectual Origins of the Jewish State,* New York: Basic Books, 1981.

Bein, Alex. *The Return to the Soil: A History of Jewish Settlement in Israel.* Jerusalem: Youth and Hechalutz Department of the Zionist Organization, 1952.

Bellerose, Ryan. "Israel: The World's First Modern Indigenous State." *Arutz Sheva*, January 14, 2014. http://www.israelnationalnews.com/Articles/Article.aspx/14377#.UtatRvunWkz

———. "Native, Jewish Blood Thicker Than Water." *Toronto Sun*, June 16, 2013. http://www.torontosun.com/2013/06/14/native-jewish-bond-thicker-than-water

———. "Why the Jews are Indigenous to Israel." YouTube, March 6, 2016. https://www.youtube.com/watch?v=v6k1gugifwA

Chacon, Richard J., and Rubén G. Mendoza, eds. *North American Indigenous Warfare and Ritual Violence*. Tucson: University of Arizona Press, 2007.

Clyne, Corrine. "How Israel Changed My Life." *The Times of Israel*, September 1, 2013. http://blogs.timesofisrael.com/how-israel-changed-my-life/

Corwin, Jay, "Native American Academics Do Not Endorse the Boycott of Israeli Academics." *The Times of Israel*, December 25, 2013. http://blogs.timesofisrael.com/native-american-academics-do-not-endorse-the-boycott-of-israeli-academics/

Courey Toensing, Gale. "Redwashing Panel Follows Academic Council's Boycott of Israel." AUB. American University of Beirut. November 31, 2013. http://indiancountrytodaymedianetwork.com/2013/12/31/redwashing-panel-follows-academic-associations-boycott-israel-152930

Deger, Allison. "Poet Joy Harjo Responds to Boycott Demands over Israeli Performance by Adding a West Bank Visit." *Mondoweiss*, December 12, 2012. http://mondoweiss.net/2012/12/poet-joy-harjo-responds-to-boycott-demands-over-israeli-performance-by-adding-a-west-bank-visit.html

Elberg, N., J. Hyman, K. Hyman, and R.F. Salisbury, *Not by Bread Alone: The Use of Subsistence Resources Among James Bay Cree*. Montreal: McGill University, Department of Sociology and Anthropology, Programme in the Anthropology of Development, 1975.

Erlich, Avi, and Victor Erlich. *Ancient Zionism: The Biblical Origins of the National Idea*. New York: Free Press, 1994.

Fuchs, Donny. "We Are NOT Indigenous." *The Jewish Press*, March 3, 2016. http://www.jewishpress.com/indepth/columns/fuchs-focus/263683/2016/03/03/

Response to Fuchs article by: Bellerose, Ryan. "Response to a Poorly Conceived Article." *Israellycool*, March 3, 2016. http://www.-israellycool.com/2016/03/03/response-to-a-poorly-conceived-article/

Harner, Michael J. *The Jivaro: People of the Sacred Waterfalls*. Berkeley: University of California Press, 1984.

Hertzberg, Arthur. *The Zionist Idea: A Conceptual Analysis and Reader*. New York: Atheneum, 1959.

Jenness, Diamond. *The Indians of Canada*. 7th Edition (Canadian University Paperbooks) Toronto: University of Toronto Press, Scholarly Publishing Division, 1977.

Joffe, Alex. "Palestinian Settler Colonialism." BESA, September 3, 2017. https://besacenter.org/perspectives-papers/palestinians-settlers-colonialism/

Karsh, Efraim. *Fabricating Israeli History: The "New Historians."* London and New York: Routledge, 2000.

Krause, Aurel. *The Tlingit Indians*. Toronto: Douglas & McIntyre, 1979, original 1885.

Laqueur, Walter. *A History of Zionism*. New York: Fine Communications, 1997.

Marayati, Laila Al. "Will Palestinians Go the Way of Native Americans?" *Los Angeles Times*, April 21, 2002. http://articles.latimes.com/2002/apr/21/opinion/op-almarayati.rtf

O'Brien, Conor-Cruise. *The Siege: The Saga of Israel and Zionism*. New York: Simon and Schuster, 1986.

"Day of Dignity in South Dakota: Scenes from Crow Creek Reservations." *Islamic Relief*, June 28, 2010. http://www.irusa.org/blog/day-of-dignity-in-south-dakota-scenes-from-crow-creek-reservation/

Rasmussen, K. *Intellectual Culture of the Iglulik Eskimos* (Report of the Fifth Thule Expedition, 1921-24). (AMS Press, 1976 ed.).

Copenhagen, New York: Gyldendalske Boghandel. (original 1929)

Sachar, Howard M. *A History of Israel from the Rise of Zionism to Our Time*. New York: Alfred A. Knopf, 1998.

Soclof, Adam. "Navajo president visiting Israel on agricultural tech mission." Jewish Telegraphic Agency, December 11, 2012 https://www.jta.org/2012/12/11/israel/navajo-president-visiting-israel-on-agricultural-tech-mission

Sturtevant, William C., ed. *Handbook of North American Indians* (15 volumes) Smithsonian Institution Scholarly Press, District of Columbia.

Teveth, Shabtai. *Ben Gurion: The Burning Ground 1886-1948*. New York: Houghton Mifflin, 1987.

Teltsch, Kathleen. "Israeli Helps Navajos Make Painted Desert Bloom." *New York Times*, August 19, 1986 https://www.nytimes.com/1986/08/19/us/israeli-helps-navajos-make-painted-desert-bloom.html

Vital, David. *The Origins of Zionism*. Oxford: Oxford University Press, 1975.

Wistrich, Robert S. *Anti-Zionism and Antisemitism in the Contemporary World*. New York: Schocken, 1994.

Yeagley, David A. "American Indians Aren't Like Palestinians." *Badeagle.com*, April 9, 2002. http://www.israelnationalnews.com/Articles/Article.aspx/1731

Zipperstein, Steven J. *Elusive Prophe: Ahad Ha'Am and the Origins of Zionism*. Berkeley: University California Press, 1993.

www.ingramcontent.com/pod-product-compliance
Lightning Source LLC
Chambersburg PA
CBHW061758110426
42742CB00012BB/1942